TREASURE BASKETS AND HEURISTIC PLAY

Ideas for children from six months to seven years

Sally Featherstone

FEATHERSTONE
IMPRINT OF BLOOMSBURY
__.,DON NEW DELHI NEW YORK SYDNEY

Published 2013 by Featherstone, an imprint of Bloomsbury Publishing plc
50 Bedford Square, London, WC1B 3DP
www.bloomsbury.com

ISBN 978-1-4081-7583-5

Text © Sally Featherstone 2013

Photographs with kind permission of:
Oak House Nursery, Brampton Abbots, Ross-on-Wye, Herefordshire;
The Cottage Kindergarten, Braeholm, 31 East Montrose Street, Helensburgh,
Scotland (Nursery World UK Nursery of the Year 2012);
Sue Gascoigne, founder of Play to Z Ltd, specialist providers of award-winning
Treasure Baskets and Sensory Play resources (www.playtoz.co.uk)

Typeset by Fakenham Prepress Solutions, Fakenham, Norfolk NR21 8NN
Printed in Great Britain by CPI Group (UK), Croydon, CR0 4YY

10 9 8 7 6 5 4 3 2 1

This book is produced using paper that is made from wood grown in
managed, sustainable forests. It is natural, renewable and recyclable.
The logging and manufacturing processes conform to the environmental
regulations of the country of origin.

To see our full range of titles visit www.bloomsbury.com

Contents

About Heuristic Play

Who is this book for?

This book has been written for anyone interested in heuristic play and the use of treasure baskets. It will be useful to you if you are:

- already familiar with heuristic play, and perhaps have used some of the activities in your setting. This book will help you to expand what you do, to ensure that you and your colleagues are clear about the processes involved, and to explain it to others.
- considering the benefits of including heuristic play for the children you work with. Here you will find information that will help you to make your decision. You can explore the benefits of heuristic play, and find details of how you could incorporate it in your work.
- exploring heuristic play as a student or for personal professional development. You will find background information on where the practice originated, and how it has developed.
- a parent or practitioner, wanting to know what to put in a basket for your baby. You will find lists of objects and advice on collecting and presenting these.

What is heuristic play?

Heuristic play is an activity where the objects, timing and organisation are clearly defined and adult led, but the play is free and belongs to the child. It is a truly 'child-chosen' activity, where the child selects and manipulates objects freely chosen from a range offered by the adult. In its *pure* sense is only really applicable to the age range from 12 months to about two and a half, although play with natural, open-ended materials and objects can and should continue throughout childhood.

In daycare settings, practitioners usually offer heuristic play in two forms:

- Treasure baskets for babies once they can sit safely on their own or securely propped.
- Heuristic play objects for older toddlers, once they are on the move, and less willing to sit and become absorbed in a basket.

The use of baskets, collections and bags of items is a permanent feature of many settings and schools, offering older children opportunities to explore, create and imagine, continuing to have pleasure from what is sometimes described as 'loose parts' play.

What is the difference between the activities?

Treasure baskets are collections of everyday objects, presented in a basket with strong sides, which the baby can access easily. The objects are all made from natural materials (wood, stone, shell, metal, bristle, leather and bone) and may also include fruit, nuts, large seeds and other natural objects. The use of artificial materials such as plastic is discouraged. A key factor of the contents of a classic treasure basket is the wide range of objects, and the individual basket usually only contains one of each type of object. Settings committed to treasure basket work often have several baskets, so babies can concentrate on them with without disturbance, and with just one baby at each basket.

Treasure basket sessions are planned and timetabled within the nursery session. Babies are offered basket work at a specific time and in a quiet place, and are given free access to the objects, selecting and discarding them as they choose. Because the babies are not mobile, they will often play undisturbed for long periods of time, and many settings offer treasure basket play for periods of between 30 minutes and an hour, observing the babies carefully, and intervening when they lose interest. Once the treasure baskets have been introduced, practitioners report that babies will play for up to an hour with the contents, showing impressive powers of concentration

as they explore the objects, returning to favourite objects again and again, and sometimes playing for long periods with a single item.

Heuristic play is less commonly used in settings, but where it is, practitioners say that it suits toddlers perfectly! It is particularly successful for two-year-olds, ideally suited to their growing independence and need to be in control of their own play. Unlike treasure basket work, heuristic play with objects needs big collections of a range of everyday objects, and once you have the objects, the activity is completely child-led. Again, children will often spend long periods of time playing individually, or less often with others, with the objects offered. The heuristic play objects include everyday things such as wooden pegs, lengths of chain, tins, cardboard tubes, hair rollers, plastic bangles, bottle and jar tops, corks and so on.

Collections are kept in separate drawstring bags, and a few bags are selected for each play session. The importance of this activity is that children have access to a large quantity, as well as a range of different objects, and this certainly helps to reduce friction between children of this age, who often grab things from each other, resulting in unacceptable behaviour. In this provision, there is plenty of everything for every child.

Heuristic play for older children

There is now plenty of evidence that heuristic play has continuing value for children throughout the Foundation Stage and well into the primary years. Collections of objects, carefully selected and offered in both adult-led and child-initiated sessions, indoors and outside,  can build on the experience of treasure baskets, supporting:

- creativity and imagination
- thinking skills
- manipulative skills
- preparation and recall of visits and visitors
- communication and language development
- story recall and story telling
- topics and themes
- children's individual interests and fascinations.

In the following chapters, you will find further information on the process of using both treasure baskets and heuristic play with babies and young children. You will also find chapters which explore the benefits of heuristic play for children throughout the early years from six months to seven years. Of course, the materials, the provision and the adult role will develop and change as children mature, so this book also gives guidance on how heuristic play itself should change to meet the needs of children at different stages of development.

The role of the adult in both treasure basket and objects work with babies and toddlers is to select and present the objects, then to sit and watch the child as they play, providing 'friendly company and emotional anchorage'. As this type of play develops through the early years, there is a place for the adult in contributing to the discussions and activities, although the children's choices, voices and thoughts should always lead the activity. Further information on the role of the adult is also included.

Why is heuristic play important?

A heuristic experience enables a person to 'discover or learn something for themself', and for babies and children this is central to the way they learn.

Jean Jacques Rousseau, in his book *Emile* was one of the earliest promoters of the need to teach children through the use of nature, natural objects and growing things:

'Teach your scholar to observe the phenomena of nature; you will soon rouse his curiosity, but if you would have it grow, do not be in too great a hurry to satisfy this curiosity. Put the problems before him and let him solve them himself. Let him know nothing because you have told him, but because he has learnt it for himself. Let him not be taught science, let him discover it. If ever you substitute authority for reason he will cease to reason; he will be a mere plaything of other people's thoughts.'

Jean-Jacques Rousseau, *Emile* (Penguin)

Other great educators, including Friedrich Froebel and Maria Montessori also believed that first-hand, immediate experiences, particularly using natural materials, would leave a lasting effect in the brain and the body, and would encourage a wide range of physical and explorative skills. Early work in this area was quickly adopted by practitioners wherever early education was developed, and is still a cornerstone of good practice.

Natural, unrestricted play, familiar to parents and early years practitioners *is* heuristic in one sense – it is the way children of all ages discover the world naturally, and we are used to seeing this sort of play in all cultures and all countries. Some examples of this natural heuristic play are:

- the games children play, alone or with friends, with stones, shells, leaves and sticks in gardens, woods and at the beach
- baby play with familiar objects at home, such as saucepans, cutlery, even the contents of their mother's handbag
- the way a small child will play for long periods of time with objects such as bottle tops, clothes pegs or buttons, putting these in containers, tipping, filling, emptying, stirring and sorting
- the play of children in back gardens, streets, fields and adventure playgrounds with planks, logs, rope, old wheels, bits of metal and other found objects, making dens, shelters and hideouts
- children in all countries and cultures using sticks, tyres, old rags and stones used to make games, dolls and other toys.

This informal play, which engages babies and children at home or during extended play in early years settings, particularly out of doors, is familiar to us all. We all have experiences we could share, for example, of children who have collected and then organised a bucket of seashells, arranging and rearranging them, absorbed in the texture, colour and pattern, exploring and comparing size and shape; or the careful, complex placing of leaves, stones, flowers and grass to form an outdoor tea-party. Babies and children will play for long periods with 'real' objects such as saucepans, tins and packets, brushes and combs, clothes pegs or cutlery. Scientists now know that experience of natural materials, and time to explore them will encourage brain growth and help children to prepare for and consolidate learning in many aspects. Such experiential learning gives essential preparation for the structured learning children undertake later in their lives, also offering time to practise and reinforce physical and mental skills.

Personal skills of concentration and perseverance, physical skills of co-ordination and fine motor management, thinking skills of problem solving and deduction are all nurtured when babies and children have free access to natural materials and long periods of time to handle and investigate them.

Recently, as more babies and children have had the benefits of early childhood provision out of their homes, they are in danger of missing the contact with natural materials that previous generations enjoyed – the open door to the garden, the regular walk to the park, the pram under the apple tree or just the blue sky. In all these experiences children heard, saw, touched, smelled and tasted all sorts of natural materials: the cold metal of the swing, the touch of the breeze on their cheeks, the texture of a leaf or a feather or the sensation of a stick poked in a puddle. All these played a vital role in expanding children's knowledge of the world around them. Early years settings and schools can become so distracted by the need to be clean and safe that they become dangerously sterile, leaving babies and children in an environment of brightly-coloured plastic toys and educational equipment, where natural materials are missing.

Of course, we need to keep children safe, but we also have a responsibility to expand their horizons and help them to explore natural materials in a natural way. The 'Loose Parts' movement is part of this, believing that babies and children need environments rich in objects from the real world, which they can select and play with, exploring and inventing, concentrating and expanding their minds. Simon Nicholson, an architect

looking at how to design effective places for people developed his well referenced theory of loose parts based on his observations of children at play on a beach. He said:

> 'In any environment, both the degree of inventiveness and creativity, and the possibility of discovery, are directly proportional to the number and kind of variables in it.'

Nicholson, S., 'How Not To Cheat Children: The theory of loose parts'
Landscape Architecture, v62, (1971)

These variables are 'loose parts' – beaches, woods and gardens have hundreds, a television set has none!

> 'Kids really get to know the environment if they can dig it, beat it, swat it, lift it, push it, join it, combine different things with it.'

Ibid

Why are natural materials used?

There is now plenty of evidence that children respond in a different and enhanced way to natural materials, such as stone, cork, wood and metal, and objects made from these. At all ages, babies and children concentrate and become much more creative with these materieals than when they are offered plastics and other manufactured toys. Good examples are the child who plays for hours with the box, ignoring the gift it contained, or the toddler absorbed in play with the tins and packets in the kitchen cupboard. There are several probable reasons for this:

- The textures of natural materials appear to be more calming and more interesting than those of smooth plastics – think of the silky grain of a wooden carving, the smooth shiny surface of a shell, the cool and flexible sensation as you handle a length of metal chain, the texture of a piece of velvet or a small sheepskin.
- The colours of natural objects are more varied and interesting than the bright primary colours of many educational toys, and these colours seem to engage children more deeply – think of the range of shades in leaves, bark, feathers and stones.
- Natural objects are much more open-ended, offering more possibilities than plastics and other manufactured educational toys which often have a single or more limited use – think of the possibilities of little containers and objects to put in them, the endless ways of building and balancing with corks or off-cuts of wood, or pretending with real-life equipment from home.
- Many objects and toys for babies and young children have been manufactured to appeal to adults, the people who buy them! – they are brightly coloured, smooth and easy to clean. Babies and children will often prefer to play with the contents of a handbag or a kitchen drawer, and the play will be much more imaginative!
- Many educational toys can only be used for one purpose – the plastic posting box, the stacking cups, the rattle. Real-life objects, such as kitchen and bathroom equipment, boxes, tins, chains or ribbon will offer more opportunities for creativity and babies and children will engage for long periods with these objects, placing and rearranging them, putting them in containers, balancing them and manipulating them, often using different

parts of their bodies. The objects and activities stimulate mirror neurons in children's brains as they imitate what they have seen others do.

What is the role of the adult?

The role of the adult in these situations is a complex and sensitive one, and often the quality of the play will be richer if the adult is *not* directly involved, but an interested bystander. As adults we tend to impose structure and limitations on children's freedom, making the game ours, not theirs, and encouraging them to play in the ways we know, rather than creating and inventing their own play.

For this reason, settings that aspire to the highest quality of heuristic play try to ensure that the adults are present but not dominant, remaining visible and showing interest, but not involving themselves in the play unless the child becomes distressed or tired. Of course, this does not mean that the adults are doing nothing! Whether the children are working with treasure baskets, bags of objects, or collections, the adults are concentrating on the play, and often use the time to make deep observations of individual babies and children. Heuristic play presents a window into the interests and preoccupations of individuals, and gives many clues to their current stage of development.

The other, and equally important role of the practitioner is the selection and presentation of the play materials. Well-selected and properly maintained baskets and other collections will ensure that the play is of high quality, engaging, interesting and fascinating to the babies and children who experience it.

This book will help you to manage the balance between being present and interfering. Of course, there are times when adult support and even direction are vital to the success of the activity, enriching and extending the play, particularly once children enter nursery or the first years of school. However true heuristic play is led and managed by the child themselves – a truly child-initiated activity.

As children get older, there are many sorts of child-led heuristic play that children will engage in informally. In high-quality settings, practitioners provide wooden blocks and other wooden toys, they ensure that every child has an opportunity for daily outdoor activities using natural materials, and they offer as many open-ended resources, both indoors and outside as they can manage.

The commitment to problem solving, critical thinking and creativity is promoted in government policies in many countries, and we look with admiration at the work of those settings where children spend the entire day out of doors. The Secret Garden Nursery in Fife, and the Forest School movement are examples of such provision. These philosophies all have central elements of heuristic play, of children discovering for themselves.

The work of Elinor Goldschmeid

Elinor Goldschmeid started a whole movement by declaring that there is a place for more concentrated and purposeful heuristic play activities for babies and children, particularly where they are in group care for much of the day. When practitioners talk about heuristic play, Elinor Goldschmeid's name is often mentioned. Her work in describing and promoting the use of heuristic play has ensured that such  play remains central to high-quality provision throughout the world, and particularly in Europe. The following text is taken from Sonia Jackson's obituary:

> 'Elinor Goldschmied, who died in 2009, at the age of 98, was one of the pioneers of early childhood care and education. The three most important new ideas that she introduced into early years practice were the treasure basket, heuristic play and the key person system, described in People Under Three (1994), co-authored with Sonia Jackson.
>
> Elinor Goldschmeid was brought up in rural Gloucestershire, the fourth of seven children, and her early life in the countryside was full of opportunities for unrestricted play. Following the death of her mother, she was sent to live with her grandfather in Bristol. Later, Elinor trained as a

nursery teacher at the Froebel Institute. She worked at Dartington Hall, the "progressive" school in Devon for five years, and in the 1930s she qualified as a psychiatric social worker.

During the second world war, Elinor Goldschmeid was asked to take responsibility for a group of evacuated children who were considered "unbilletable" because of their wild behaviour, and this provided the foundation for much of her later work on the management and organisation of day nurseries, both in Britain and Italy.

In 1946, she went back to Italy with her Italian husband, to work with young children in a home for single mothers in Milan, and her work influenced the transformation of childcare in Italy. From this experience she wrote a book, Il Bambino nell'Asilo Nido (The Child in the Nursery), one of the first books to address the group care of very young children.

After her husband's death in 1955, she returned to England, working as an education social worker in London, and, following her formal retirement, she began a new career as a consultant in several London boroughs and in Italy, work she continued into her nineties.

She produced eight documentary films describing how advances in our understanding of child development can be applied in everyday practice. But perhaps her major contribution came through her inspired teaching of generations of early years workers. All who met her were profoundly influenced. Largely by word of mouth, her ideas have spread far beyond the childcare centres where she taught directly, and will continue to do so for many years to come.'

Distilled from Sonia Jackson's obituary for Elinor Goldschmeid, *The Observer* (12 June 2009)

Elinor Goldschmeid's book *People Under Three*, written with Sonia Jackson, was first published in 1994, and is still a bestseller in early years education. It has been in print ever since, recently in an updated edition. The book describes her work in her nursery setting, providing guidance on all aspects of daycare. The book was supported by video footage of heuristic play in action, and these have now been converted to DVD format.

Two principles

At the centre of the Goldschmeid model for planned heuristic play are two major principles, which make it different from more familiar forms of first-hand play, and remain at the heart of the activity:

1   The objects used, which have been selected by the adult, and are presented during a session where other toys and equipment are not available – therefore offering no choice of *what* to play with beyond those resources offered in the session. The freedom for the child is in *how* they explore and play with the collection objects offered.
2   The role of the supporting adult, which, unlike other parts of the session or day, is confined to preparing the activity, selecting the resources and then sitting near the child or children as they play, showing interest, but with no intervention role, apart from helping a child who may be distressed, or using body language and words to encourage the child to remain engaged with the play. This may prove difficult for practitioners who are used to being very involved in play, where babies and children have great freedom in what they play with, and the adult role is to support and extend this play.

Together, these closely defined features of heuristic play have an effect that is very different from more unstructured play, focusing babies' and children's concentration and enabling them to explore objects and their own responses to them in great depth. Anyone thinking of embarking on this model should be very clear about the differences as well as the similarities. The advantages are many, but the method must be understood in its entirety.

Some settings have deliberately adapted their approach to heuristic play, either by changing the role of the adult to a much more proactive one, or by incorporating resources that are not made from natural materials, and this can dilute the purity and the effect of the activity.

It is also very important to remember that Elinor Goldschmeid did not expect heuristic play with objects or treasure baskets to take up the majority of the day or the session. It was always expected to be only one part of the provision, offered frequently (daily in many settings) but not displacing other activities where the child's choice and the role of the adult are very different.

The pure method

The children Elinor Goldschmeid worked with were offered heuristic play in two major ways, and these have been incorporated into early years practice in the UK and in many other countries, where practitioners and teachers plan and provide for specific sessions of this type of play.

1. Treasure basket work

This was provided for babies who could sit unaided or securely propped, but were not yet mobile. It is difficult to put an exact age range here, as babies develop at very different rates. Elinor Goldschmeid was aware that at this stage, the baby is awake for longer periods, beginning to be interested in the wider world, but not able to move unaided, and their frustration was often evident as babies grizzled, reached out and generally demanded the attention of their carers. Her solution was to provide a basket of objects selected from familiar environments, safe to use, and made from natural materials, and the classic treasure basket was born.

The babies were offered the objects in a basket, placed next to where they were seated or securely propped, so they could reach into the basket and select objects to explore. The babies were free to choose which objects they played with and there were never more than two babies using each basket, usually one basket was provided for each baby. This pure form of play has been described as the first truly 'self-chosen' activity.

Since its invention, work with treasure baskets has been extended to children of all ages who have additional needs, particularly those who are less mobile or who have severe learning or physical difficulties. More recently there has been a strong move in some schools and settings to extend work with treasure baskets and other heuristic play into the programmes for older children. These baskets of objects are often linked to children's current interests, or to aspects of learning. Guidance on these 'themed' baskets, and the use of heuristic play for older children, is included in Chapter 5 (see page 64).

2. Heuristic play with objects

This was the second heuristic play activity offered to the babies in Elinor Goldschmeid's nursery. This activity is less familiar, and less used in early years settings, but follows logically from treasure basket play, as it was offered to older babies and toddlers who were on the move, particularly those who were crawling and beginning to walk. Elinor Goldschmeid noticed that once

babies could move and particularly when they began to crawl or walk, they no longer wanted to play with the static basket of objects, preferring to move as they learned, carrying objects around and manipulating them, particularly combining them with containers of all sorts.

In their book, *People under Three*, Elinor Goldschmied and Sonia Jackson coined the term heuristic play, to explain how to provide a more structured opportunity for this kind of activity. Heuristic play:

> 'consists of offering a group of children, for a defined period of time in a controlled environment, a large number of different kinds of objects and receptacles with which they play freely without adult intervention'
> Elinor Goldschmeid and Sonia Jackson *People Under Three* (Routledge)

It is particularly useful for children *in their second year* who often seem unwilling to engage in any activity for more than a few minutes. Whilst the heuristic play session is in process, *adults need to remain seated and quiet*. This supports children in making their own choices and discoveries. To provide for heuristic play, practitioners collect natural materials like fir cones, conkers, seashells, and pebbles, as well as ribbons, short lengths of chain, and 'found' objects like curtain rings, jar lids, sturdy cardboard tubes, the reels from inside sticky tape, and empty cotton reels.

These older children, able and wanting to move around, were offered large quantities of objects, with containers and tubes of all sorts to put or post them into, roll or drop them through, or carry them around. At this stage of development, many children are exploring schemas such as containing, rolling, posting, arranging, filling and emptying, so the collections of objects were just what they needed to continue their explorations. The objects (bottle tops, curtain rings, corks and so on) were stored in big drawstring bags, and tipped out on to a carpeted floor for the session. Simple containers such as tins, boxes and bottles, some with slots or holes in them, were also added. The large number of items in these collections was very important, as the children were mobile and would move to the objects they wished to play with. Vital to this type of play was that there should be enough of each item for this to happen. Once the materials had been put out on the carpet, children had free access to these materials and space to explore them.

Heuristic play was always different from other planned play opportunities in the nursery. These resources were selected and presented by the adults and the sessions for play were long. Both types of play were offered several times a week and for around an hour at a time, and during these sessions, the other play activities were put away, so the children could concentrate. This may seem very structured and perhaps even restrictive, denying children choice at this time, but Elinor Goldschmeid and her staff only needed to watch the way children responded to heuristic play materials to see evidence of their enjoyment and absorption.

When this type of play was offered, Eleanor Goldschmeid advised that it should be the only activity on offer, so there was no distraction from the work in hand, and adults were available to support the work. The role of the adult in both these types of heuristic play is of organiser and observer, only intervening to prevent disruption or disagreement. In this role, the adult is in an excellent place to observe the play without guilt or interruption! As in treasure basket sessions, these long observations are very useful in identifying strengths and needs of individual children.

Both treasure basket and heuristic play are planned and offered for relatively long periods of time, at least an hour is planned, and sometimes practitioners will be flexible about extending this if children are still absorbed, as they often are.

Since the introduction of heuristic play for children 'on-the-move', practitioners, teachers and those who advise them have realised how important it is for children in the early years to have access to open-ended materials, both on their own and in combination with other learning resources. Heuristic play with objects has also been extended into work with older children, and practitioners and teachers are now offering quantities of natural and man-made 'loose parts' such as logs, planks, shells, pebbles, bottle tops, pegs and so on for free exploration.

How does heuristic play develop?

It is obvious from Elinor Goldschmeid's guidance and from the work of researchers into child development and the ways that very young children learn, that provision for heuristic play should be different at different ages and stages of development. The following chart attempts to explain the key features and differences across the range from about six months (as long as the baby can sit unaided or securely propped), to the age of about seven years.

Development stage	What the child needs in heuristic play
1. Sitting babies	At this stage, babies are interested in everything. They are practising grasping and releasing objects with their fingers and hands, twisting their wrists, waving things in the air, dropping and picking up. They are also exploring surfaces and objects with all their senses, and particularly with their mouths, which at this stage is a major organ of discovery.
	A well-filled treasure basket, stimulating to all the senses is ideal for the sitting baby. These baskets should be well maintained and filled to the brim with a range of everyday objects. At home, of course, the baby can play with the basket at any time when they need a bit of stimulation and they are not tired or hungry. In early years settings, the activity should be planned and timetabled to provide both space and time for the babies to concentrate, and should be offered several times a week. (See Chapter 2, page 27, for detailed descriptions of objects and organisation for treasure baskets for babies.)
2. Crawling, standing, toddling babies	Some toddlers may still enjoy access to a treasure basket, but you may need to review the contents once children are on the move and have more strength in their hands and arms. Large stones, lengths of chain and some kitchen implements may present hazards for older children who may be interested in throwing or banging items on surfaces or even on other children! (See Chapter 3, page 44 for detailed descriptions of objects and organisation for treasure baskets for older babies and children with additional needs.)
	However, once babies become mobile, the treasure basket may not present enough challenge for their newly found freedom. They are often single-minded and can be defiant with adults and aggressive towards other children particularly when expected to share! At this stage, children need something that fulfills their need for exploration and for movement, so heuristic play is ideal for toddlers, who have such a great need to move about and explore. Heuristic play sessions provide

a plentiful supply of materials and open-ended uses, which match the needs of two-year-olds, providing plenty of opportunities to practise the child's schemas of the moment – filling, emptying, posting, wrapping, dumping, transporting objects and so on. The activity should be planned and timetabled to provide both space and time for the children to concentrate without getting in each other's way.

(See Chapter 4, page 53, for detailed descriptions of objects and organisation for heuristic play with bags of objects for toddlers.)

3. Active young learners (age 3–4)

Treasure baskets of familiar objects may still be popular with some younger children, and are particularly useful for children with additional needs.

Heuristic play with objects can begin to extend beyond the structured session to become an element of child-initiated play and learning. Collections may be themed or follow the method used at Stage 2, although the large collections of objects will still need adult support. Outdoor heuristic play should be an integral part of provision every day.

Some small themed collections to support stories or for remembering significant experiences may be useful at this stage.

(See Chapter 5, page 64, for detailed descriptions of objects and organisation for 'loose parts' play for three to four-year-olds.)

4. Active older learners (age 5–7)

Heuristic play objects, indoors and outside should be included as part of continuous provision. Indoor provision will include quantities of natural and recycled objects, and familiar household and 'real-life' objects. Out of doors, a wider range of larger and more complex resources should now be added to the range from which children can select. Materials collected on visits and walks, recycled materials and other found and natural items can be incorporated in children's work.

Indoors and outside, adults should provide support, and extend the children's own ideas by adding new resources, often at the children's request. Adults will also introduce challenges and provocations to encourage the extension of heuristic play while preserving its place within child choice and individual response.

Baskets of objects can continue to support creativity and thinking skills, learning in topic activities, literacy and early mathematics. Adults may regularly lead sessions where baskets are introduced, with the baskets then offered as part of continuous provision. Other baskets can be stocked with objects to support the emerging interests of individuals or groups of children.

(See Chapter 5, page 64, for descriptions of objects and organisation for 'loose parts' play, and collections for older children.)

Meeting the needs of individuals and groups

When making decisions about the planning of heuristic play sessions and the objects to be offered, practitioners and teachers should consider the stage of development of the children, not just their age. It is evident from recent research into child development that some groups and individuals may be hindered in their development if the programme does not match their current needs, and particularly when it is planned for their chronological age, not their stage of development.

As children grow older, the following groups may need provision from either the stage before or the stage after the rest of the group:

- The youngest children in the group (often referred to as 'summer born') may need to continue longer with free-choice heuristic play or to have more large object play out of doors.
- Children with exceptional ability in one area of the curriculum, and who often show a passion for certain objects, activities or play subjects may need specific resources tailored to these needs and interests and may be very inventive when using such open-ended materials.
- Some older children, often girls, are cautious about very open-ended activities, and may need more adult support and modelling in order to get involved in heuristic play. Their needs may be best met by small-scale heuristic play with objects, such as miniature environments, collections of smaller natural objects, or combining heuristic materials with malleable materials or characters to inspire their involvement. These children may also benefit from small collections of objects linked to their own experiences or to a familiar story or place.

- Some children, often boys, are developmentally less advanced, and may enjoy simpler activities, such as a 'familiar object' treasure basket, for longer.
- Some boys have problems with fine-motor skills and may need more space or structure than other children, often favouring object play outside or in larger spaces.
- Children with additional needs can benefit from the sensory experiences of heuristic play, and treasure baskets can include objects of reference specific to the particular child. Contents of these treasure baskets should include objects that stimulate all the senses, particularly the senses of sound, touch and smell.
- Children with English as an Additional Language, or those who do not speak English often benefit greatly from heuristic play. The open-ended nature of the materials means they are culturally free of bias, and can be used to play out or explore without the need for extended communication skills.
- Children experiencing stressful situations, such as refugees, asylum seekers, or those subject to abuse, often find comfort in play with open-ended materials as they play out their experiences or use fantasy as a release.

How do I plan the sessions?

If you are thinking of introducing heuristic play into your setting, you will need to make a commitment to the time and space it will inevitably take. The discussion of the *when*, *where* and *what with*, as well as the *who* and the *why*, will take time, but this discussion and agreement is essential. Everyone must be on board with the decision, because if they are not, the initiative will not succeed.

As children become more familiar with heuristic play, and more physically capable of managing the objects, the sessions will change, both in time and place. Of course, babies will be working closely in very small groups, probably with their own key person, and the sessions will be closely planned and always accompanied by an adult (ideally each baby's own key person). As children mature and become more mobile, the play should still be planned to ensure the maximum space and that most of the adults are present.

For younger babies

Treasure baskets for the younger babies should be planned several times every week, and sufficient time should be allowed for the babies to get really involved in the contents of the baskets. Most settings find that, as long as the objects are interesting and varied, and the adults are in view, babies can and do concentrate for long periods  on this activity, and many settings allow between 45 minutes and an hour, with practitioners available to support or accompany any baby who becomes bored or distressed.

Treasure basket times should be incorporated into the session plan and take place at a time and in a place where there are few interruptions or distractions. For this reason, many settings have several baskets available, so there are never more than two babies at each basket. Other nursery activities are not available during this time.

For older babies and toddlers

Heuristic play for older babies and toddlers should also be planned for times and spaces where distractions and interruptions are less likely. Settings where this play is offered will timetable sessions for twice or three times every week, and for about an hour, including getting out the materials, and the collecting and putting away of these by the children.

This commitment of time is particularly important for heuristic play with objects, which should take place in as large a space as possible, and for all the children in the group at the same time. This is to reduce the possibilities for the activity to become diffuse, for the objects to 'disappear' and become incorporated in the general resources of the setting, and for the children to be able to concentrate without distractions.

For older children

It has been said by researchers that, in order for their brains to develop, and for them to practise the skills they are currently developing, children need to spend about a third of their time on self-chosen activities, such as heuristic play. Practitioners and teachers would do well to take note of this research, particularly at a time when children start formal education at ever earlier ages, spend more and more of their time in directed activities, and less and less time out of doors or in free play.

As children become more independent, and particularly in Reception classes and in Key Stage 1, the number of adults available to model, promote and value heuristic play will vary, and will probably never be as favorable as in a baby room. However, there should be an adult available to the children in any continuous provision, and this includes heuristic play activities, although the adult may well be available for other activities at the same time.

For older children the nature of continuous provision will mean that heuristic play can be offered continuously too. The range and nature of the objects should change over time and according to the children's interests, to maintain interest and spark enthusiasms, but opportunities to use these open-ended materials should be a permanent feature both indoors and outside.

Practitioners and teachers will need to decide on the exact organisation after observing the needs and developmental stages of the children in their group, and the organisation should be flexible enough to adapt over time as the children mature.

Further guidance on storage and resources can be found in Chapter 6, see page 103.

How do I organise the sessions?

Treasure basket sessions for younger babies should take the following into account:

- **Storage of materials** – depending on the space available, the treasure baskets can be stored full, on a high shelf or in a cupboard, or empty, with the contents of each basket hung in plastic or cloth bags on hooks. The important thing to remember is that the treasure basket contents are *not* for general use, or they will become lost or otherwise unavailable for this important activity. Every member of staff should be made aware of the importance of their role in protecting these materials.
- **The baskets** – these should be deep enough to hold a wide range of objects, wide enough to be stable when leaned on, and sturdy enough to stand up to frequent use. (See the photographs in Chapter 7, page 108.)
- **Quantity of resources** – the baskets should be full to the brim with a wide range of items, usually one of each. The secret of a good treasure basket experience is for the baby to have a great range of things to choose from. We can't ever know what will engage a particular baby, all we can do is provide a good choice of things. If you are not sure whether you have got it right, look at the basket yourself and see what attracts you.
- **Quality of the objects** – a high quality treasure basket doesn't need to be expensive, and you don't need to buy everything on the list. However, the things you collect should be the best you can find. They don't need to be new, but they do need to be of good quality and in good condition. Everything should be checked regularly for damage. Fresh items such as fruit and paper items should be checked, removed when past their best, and replaced with new ones. As many babies will put objects in their mouths, baskets and their contents should also be cleaned regularly. Further guidance on safety and hygiene is included in Chapter 6, see page 103.
- **Space** – there should be enough space for each baby to explore their own basket without interference from others. This may involve you in moving some other objects or furniture to make enough space. If you choose to have two babies at each basket, make sure the basket is big enough, and that they are seated at opposite sides. Shared baskets may need more adult support.
- **Position** – babies should be seated or propped securely so they are alongside the basket. The baby should be able to lean on the edge of the basket with their arm, and reach the objects in the basket.
- **Distractions** – other play materials should be put away or covered up during this time, or the babies should sit in a quiet area away from the more active

areas of the nursery. Practitioners should sit quietly where the babies can see them, allowing the babies to feel secure and to concentrate.

Heuristic play for older babies and toddlers should take the following into account:

- **Storage of the materials** – resources are traditionally stored in drawstring fabric bags hung on hooks in a cupboard or on the wall of the setting.
- **Quantity of resources** – the resources for heuristic play at this stage should be plentiful. Eleanor Goldschmeid suggests that there should be between 50 and 60 items in each bag. One setting in Barcelona has collected 36 different bags, with 60 items in each bag! Of course, you shouldn't wait until you have this number of bags before you start your first session, but the children do need enough variety for each session and enough variety over a number of sessions to maintain their interest. A good starter set is 15 bags with 60 items in each bag. There is a list of items you could collect on page 109.
- **Resources for each session** – in each session the practitioner is advised to offer about five different sorts of resource (five bags), together with enough containers (tins, boxes etc) for two or three per child.
- **Space** – there should be enough space for the children to explore the objects you offer them without interference from others. This may involve you in moving objects or furniture to make enough space.
- **Position** – the guidance is to place containers at intervals round the space, with objects from each bag in separate piles, where the children can help themselves.
- **Distractions** – other play materials should be put away or covered up during this time, and practitioners should sit quietly where the babies and toddlers can see them, allowing them to feel secure and to concentrate. Adults should

be ready to intervene if there are disputes, or to work alongside any child who appears distressed or does not get involved.

Heuristic play for older nursery children, and those in Reception and Key Stage 1 (up to seven years old) should take the following into account:

- **Resources for each session** – at this developmental stage, heuristic play with objects increasingly becomes an element of continuous provision, so the resources will be available for the long periods during which continuous provision is offered. It is important to remember that children need enough variety and enough  choice of where and what to play with to enable them to follow their interests and take on the provocations and challenges you present them with. You may also decide to offer new or different resources from time to time to extend and expand their thinking and creativity. Early years practitioners and teachers are renowned for their ability to collect objects for play, and these objects sometimes come about by chance, providing unique opportunities for creativity.

- **Storage of materials for continuous use** – the storage of resources for continuing heuristic play is a constant issue and a vital key to its success. The older children get, the more choice and control they should have over the objects for this type of play. Every room is different, and those of you with restricted space will need to think carefully about the range of objects you can offer, how often these are changed and how they are stored. A smaller range of carefully-selected and easily-accessible resources presented in sorting trays, small baskets or a trolley, will produce more effective play, particularly if these are replaced regularly with new types of objects. Jumbled boxes of mixed resources will not promote purposeful play, so practitioners and teachers will need to look at the balance between organisation and range, selecting a balance that suits their provision.

- **Quantity of resources** – the resources for heuristic play at this stage should be plentiful, but the need for very large quantities of each will reduce over time, partly because the activity is unlikely to involve the whole group at once, and because the children will hopefully be more willing to work together, to share resources, and to discuss differences of opinion. Your continuous provision will also offer other activities such as sand, water, construction and so on, which will reduce the demand on heuristic materials.

- **Access to the resources** – heuristic play at this stage needs to be an independent activity, where children can get the things they need, rather than a specific 'timetabled' session. This will present challenges, but the essential rule is to make the resources visible (for example in clear containers), well organised (so children can find and return them), in good condition (clean, undamaged) and varied (so children have a real choice of inspiring resources). The essence of the activity is to explore objects and their properties, not to produce a finished object, so the resources do not get 'used up' and are returned to their containers at the end of the session.

- **Space** – there should be enough space for the children to explore the objects you offer them without interference from others. The organisation of your room should reflect the need for children to work with heuristic materials, ensuring there is enough space indoors and outside for this activity. Builders' trays, small mats, carpet squares, plant saucers, boards and other surfaces will help to define spaces, particularly for small or fragile creations. A digital camera is essential so children can record their own work in the spaces you offer. Heuristic play is often a temporary feature of children's play, a thing of the moment which needs to be captured, and for many children, photography will turn their play from ephemera into a more permanent memory. Their photos will also give you an opportunity to value heuristic play by including it in children's records and in feedback or plenary sessions.

- **Distractions** – unlike earlier stages of development, at this stage most children will be able to concentrate on their own play and creations when other activities are also going on. Plenty of practice and a real sense of power over their own learning will help children to concentrate on their own activities. Genuine free choice supports this ability to concentrate, as children who have chosen *what*, *where* and *who* to play with for at least a part of each day will concentrate better, both during this time and when they are asked to join more adult-directed sessions.

- **The role of the adult** – you will need to balance free-access play with adults available, and sessions where adults may introduce object collections linked to specific aspects of learning, recent experiences or particular interests raised by the children.

- **The use of collections of objects** – these will probably be collected by the teachers/practitioners in advance of the adult-led session. The collection, once discussed in a group, is usually left for the children to explore independently for a time, as part of continuous provision. Collections of this sort are temporary enhancements to provision.

How do the resources change as children develop?

Development stage	Treasure basket work	Heuristic play with objects
Sitting babies	Sitting babies need treasure baskets filled to the brim with a wide range of real-life objects: • natural materials – including wood, leather, metal, glass, fabric, bristle, cane, rubber, paper, card • familiar items from the home – including fruit, kitchen implements, brushes, containers, boxes • objects from nature– including shells, stones, pebbles, feathers (For a full list see page 110 and for suppliers of suitable baskets see Chapter 7, page 109.)	
Crawling, standing, toddling babies	Treasure baskets may still be offered to toddlers, and their contents will remain much the same, although their need to be on the move may limit their interest! However, while a basket for babies may contain some larger, heavy, or potentially risky objects (because babies' wrists are not strong enough for them to do any damage by throwing or hitting with them), you will need to check the baskets when using them with older children, particularly those who are interested in throwing or hitting with objects. Suggestions for baskets to support schemas can be found on pages 47.	For heuristic play toddlers will need: • a minimum of ten drawstring fabric bags, each containing a large number of one sort of object, for example, corks, card tubes, hair rollers, bangles, metal jar caps, wooden 'dolly' pegs, table tennis balls, woollen pompoms, wooden egg cups, wooden balls • containers for children to use in play, for example, little metal or wooden bowls, card or wooden boxes, empty tins (For a full list see Chapter 4, page 59.)

Active young learners (age 3–4)	Treasure baskets of familiar objects may still appeal to some children, and these can be themed to link to projects or to support individual interests. Suggestions for baskets to support sensory play and children's interests can be found in Chapter 2, see page 27.	Heuristic play should be supported beyond the structured sessions by some of the following: • access to heuristic play bags during child-initiated learning sessions • boxes or baskets of these items offered near sand, water and construction play • heuristic play sessions out of doors on rugs, tents or in big trays • practitioners who source, collect and offer heuristic play items, such as seasonal objects – leaves, conkers, shells – in large quantities for creative play. (See Chapter 5, page 66 for further details.)
Active older learners (age 5–7)	At this stage, the range of heuristic and other open-ended play materials should continue, and children should have free access to these in their play, both outdoors and inside. They should also be encouraged to collect objects themselves to add to the collections in their classrooms. Heuristic play objects should be returned, sorted and stored by the children after play, so they can be re-used. At this stage baskets of objects can have a wide variety of uses, suggestions for 'loose parts' play, and for specific collections of objects for discussion are detailed in Chapter 5, see page 66.	

In further Chapters of this book you will find more detailed guidance on the particular provision for each stage of development, including:

- treasure basket work (Chapter 1, page 12 and Chapter 2, page 32)
- focused heuristic play sessions (Chapter 3, page 44)
- incorporating 'loose parts' experiences into your work with older children (Chapter 5, page 64).

Heuristic Play for Younger Babies: The Treasure Basket

What are babies like at this stage, and what do they need?

Babies develop at different rates, and the age at which babies and children reach developmental milestones is very varied, even for those who don't have illnesses or additional needs. This is due to lots of different factors – genetic makeup, environmental factors, health, nutrition, cultural expectations and even how much encouragement they get! These factors have an effect throughout childhood, and will result in wide-ranging differences in the age at which babies and children reach the milestones of smiling, standing and walking, saying their first word, becoming toilet trained and sleeping through the night. Parents and practitioners watch for these milestones with great anticipation and see evidence of them with great pleasure, comparing each baby with other family members, siblings and the children of friends.

Most babies learn to sit up, either propped or unaided, at some time between six and nine months. However, it is important to add that while some babies learn to sit unaided at five months, some still can't do it securely at twelve months, and that sitting up unaided is one of the most important developmental milestones, often missed as we look for smiles, words or walking. At this point, all the head-lifting, wriggling, waving, squirming and rolling the baby has been doing will come to fruition. They have been training for this moment – a new view on the world! At last they have the strength in their back and tummy muscles to hold their trunk up, and the strength in their neck and shoulder muscles to hold their own head up, enabling them to look around as they sit. At last they can see across a room, they can see things the right way up, and most importantly, sitting up frees their fingers, hands, wrists and arms to reach, grab, hold and manipulate the objects they can reach.

Babies who are beginning to sit up and take notice are a very special group, and the milestone indicates a new stage in the baby's learning. They will never again be the dependent bundle, relying totally on adults to carry them to things or hold them up so they can see. Their hands and fingers (and their mouths) are eager to touch, taste, shake, squeeze and otherwise explore the things they can see, but they are still immobile – stuck in a sitting position until the next physical milestone of crawling. This huge achievement brings with it some frustrations and demands – how can I get hold of what I can see? The sign of that frustration is often grizzling, vocalising frantically, waving, gesturing or tears, all signs that the baby wants to communicate, but can't.

At this stage it will be obvious that adults either need to be mind-readers or to bring the world to the baby. This is where the classic treasure basket comes into its own, filled to the brim with the sort of everyday objects that babies see around them all the time, carefully selected to provide stimulation for all the senses, artfully arranged so they are ready to explore, and presented in a container that is strong enough to lean on and big enough to be exciting.

As an experienced nursery practitioner, knowledgeable about child development, and keen to respond to what she saw, Elinor Goldschmeid adopted this solution to the frustrations of the baby ready to explore, but still stuck in one place.

Principles for selecting objects for treasure baskets

There are several simple principles you should use when selecting or buying objects to include in your treasure baskets. These are based on the advice from Elinor Goldschmeid in *People Under Three* (Routledge):

- All the objects are everyday, easily-found objects.
- Everything in the basket is natural – no plastic or other man-made materials should be included. Some of the ready-filled baskets on the market contain items made from plastic and other synthetic materials. Check before you buy.
- The objects are cleaned regularly, either by washing or wiping with a clean damp cloth.
- Fruit or other natural objects, which may deteriorate, are replaced regularly.
- The objects can't be swallowed by a baby. If you aren't sure, use a choke tester from your chemist or the internet (see Chapter 7 for suppliers, page 113). The size of the Babydan choke tester is 3.5cm and the size of a kitchen roll centre is about 4.5cm, so if you can't get a choke tester, post the object down a kitchen roll tube. Anything that falls right through the hole in the tube should be discarded. If you are not sure, don't put that object in the

basket. Alternatively take this piece of advice given by Elinor Goldschmeid to a worried practitioner:

'If you think an item might be swallowed, put it in your own mouth and see if you could swallow it yourself. You will probably find it is quite impossible.' She also said '... if in doubt, throw it out!'

People Under Three (Routledge)

The basket

The ideal basket for treasure basket or object work is a shallow basket made of wicker, rush or straw, with straight sides, strong enough to lean on. It should be between 10cm and 15cm deep and not less than 35cm across.

The objects for the treasure basket are many and varied, and the suggestions here are neither compulsory nor an exhaustive list. As with all equipment and resources used with babies and young children, you must decide for yourself which objects you will put in your heuristic play collections, including those for treasure baskets. The general advice is 'if you aren't happy with any object on the list, don't put it in!'

Suitable objects for a classic treasure basket

Collecting the objects for your own treasure basket is both easy and pleasurable! Take your time, and keep adding objects as you see them.

The following list has been constructed for practitioners or parents who want to start collecting, and as a checklist for those of you with more experience. We have started the search in the home, with suggestions for things you could easily find. You will certainly be able to add more ideas:

Look around your own house, where you might find:	Look in bargain or 'pound' shops, or charity shops, where you might find:
• a small wooden spoon, fork or honey dipper	• a metal whisk
• a set of metal spoon measures	• a set of metal biscuit cutters
• a bunch of keys	• different sizes of wooden spoons
• a small metal whisk	• metal beakers
• wooden clothes pegs	• metal dishes, ash trays or bowls
• a pastry brush	• wood or metal egg cups
• a metal or wooden egg cup	• brass or wooden curtain rings

- small spoons
- little metal scoops
- a nailbrush
- a wood or glass lemon squeezer
- a small metal funnel
- a garlic press
- a bottle brush
- a pastry brush
- small cardboard boxes
- small tins with screw tops (to fill with rice, dried beans or peas)
- smooth tin lids
- strainers and small sieves
- wooden spoons and spatulas
- spaghetti measurer
- corks
- a mushroom brush
- wooden salad servers
- napkin rings
- coasters
- a mustard spoon – wood or metal
- a potato masher
- small spoons and scoops
- cardboard tubes
- clothes pegs
- little baskets
- cork or raffia mats
- a sturdy glass salt pot
- metal funnels
- empty biscuit tins
- a tea strainer or infuser
- small jam tart tins
- tissue-paper, foil, greaseproof paper
- an orange, lemon, or avocado stone

- a tea strainer or infuser
- small bells
- a shoe brush
- baby rattles (wood, cane, gourd)
- wood or metal napkin rings
- small wooden or metal bowls
- wooden bangles
- bottle brushes
- bags of shells
- hair 'scrunchies'
- wood or metal mug trees
- castanets
- a metal whistle
- a small mouth organ
- bulldog paper clips
- rubber balls
- tennis balls
- keyrings
- a tiny teddy
- marble 'eggs'
- paperweights
- 'snows storms'
- sponges
- a wooden foot or back massager
- shells
- ribbon
- lace
- big wooden beads
- small metal or wooden boxes
- a silver survival blanket
- woven netting
- small musical instruments (rattles, drums, castanets)
- little bells

Look on a walk or holiday where you might find:
- some fir cones
- shells
- smooth pebbles
- large nuts – chestnuts or walnuts
- big feathers

Look in an ironmongers or DIY store where you might find:
- lengths of chain
- decorators' paint brushes
- a chamois leather or pad
- a bicycle bell
- bath plug and chain

- big leaves

- rubber door wedges and doorstops
- wood or metal drawer and door knobs
- metal pet bowls

Look in your bedroom or bathroom, where you might find:

- an empty little perfume bottle
- a small hairbrush
- a small loofah
- a nail brush
- a make-up brush
- a comb
- a bath brush
- a toothbrush (new)
- nail buffers and large emery boards
- a clean flannel
- a glasses case
- a little leather purse
- beads on a string
- rings with big stones strung on a string or a keyring
- a handbag mirror
- a metal powder compact
- hairbands or 'scrunchies'
- small gift boxes
- a pumice stone
- emery boards

Look in a home décor or gift shop where you might find:

- sponges
- shells
- dried gourds
- small wooden or metal boxes
- string and cane balls
- wooden apples and other fruit
- little fabric gift bags
- little metal tins and wooden boxes
- cellophane paper, foil, tissue-paper
- small mirrors
- rush or raffia mats and coasters
- little baskets
- a tea infuser
- split dried oranges and lemons

Look in a hobby shop where you might find:

- small bells
- curtain rings
- ribbon
- dressing gown cord
- sequin waste
- small pieces of lace, fur fabric
- lavender bags
- wooden and marble eggs
- a darning 'mushroom'
- big wooden beads to string
- cane bag handles
- ribbon, lace and braid

- 'dolly' pegs
- corks of different sizes
- wooden spools

You could make:

- woollen pompom balls
- rag dolls
- fabric bricks or books
- small cloth bags with herbs inside
- bean bags

⇨

Planning for the treasure basket session

Of course, at home, the treasure basket can be used at any time when the baby is awake, alert and ready for play. In daycare settings, some practitioners have adopted this flexible approach and will offer treasure baskets to their key babies when they feel it is appropriate. In other settings, particular times during the session are allocated for treasure basket work. The disadvantage of this second approach is that the baby may not be ready for the basket at a predetermined time, so a more flexible approach should be used whenever possible.

Detailed guidance follows on how to make and maintain a classic treasure basket

Name: My basket
Type of collection: The classic treasure basket
Age group: Sitting babies

Introduction

This basket is based on the original version recommended by Elinor Goldschmeid. It is a varied and mixed collection of household and familiar objects, and the wide range of contents is the major attraction for babies who are able to sit and reach for the things that appeal to them. The essential element is that the basket appeals to all the senses, with a wide variety of objects, and that the baby has free choice of these, with an interested adult on hand nearby.

The contents of the basket are generally grouped under the following categories, and we have reorganised the list from page 34 in these categories to help you check the range of objects as you collect them:

- Objects made of wood
- Objects made of metal
- Natural objects
- Fabrics, paper, card
- Objects made from leather, fur, fabric, rubber and wool

The objects should also appeal to all the senses:

- Touch – a variety of textures, weights, shapes and surfaces.
  Ask yourself: *Have I found objects that are shiny, dull, rough, smooth, heavy, light, bumpy, fuzzy, prickly, slippery, cool, furry, corrugated, fibrous, bendy, silky, polished?*
- Sound – a variety of sound makers.
  Ask yourself: *Have I found objects that ring, rattle, scrunch, bang, rasp, crinkle, tinkle, swish, scratch, pop, tear?*
- Sight – things of different colours and shades, forms and shapes.
  Ask yourself: *Have I found objects of different sizes, a range of natural colours, with patterns of dots, spots, lines, spirals; things that twinkle, reflect, shine, twist, spin, roll, slide?*
- Smell – important and often missed.
  Ask yourself: *Have I found objects that remind babies of home, that smell good, herby, flowery, fruity, perfumed?*
- Taste – a bit more difficult, but still possible, and very desirable.
  Ask yourself: *Have I found objects that babies can safely mouth and suck; things that are smooth, bumpy, prickly, smooth, textured?*

It's also useful to think of adding things of different sizes and weights to your basket – babies need to be able to choose a heavy stone, a length of chain with big links, a light and easily manipulated whisk, or a feather. The heavy items are often the most popular, giving fingers, wrists and hands a work-out.

You should regularly rearrange the objects in the basket to make sure that the heavy items don't all sink to the bottom, and so the baby is aware of different contents on different occasions – but don't be tempted to put the things you like at the top! Babies should have complete freedom to choose what they are interested in.

Container

You need a classic treasure basket made from natural materials, such as straw, cane, rush, or raffia (see Chapter 7, page 110, for suppliers). Choose a sturdy basket, as the baby will be leaning on the edge, and make sure it is deep enough to contain all the items you are offering for play. The basket should be filled to the brim, and you should aim to add to the contents regularly to maintain interest.

The objects should be checked and cleaned regularly (see Chapter 6, page 105).

What to collect

Keep these thoughts in mind as you collect objects for your classic treasure basket:

- The objects are all everyday, easily-found items.
- Nothing is a bought 'toy'.
- Everything in the basket is natural – no plastic or other man-made materials.
- The objects are easily cleaned.
- Fruit and other natural objects are replaced regularly.
- The objects have been checked to make sure they can't be swallowed by babies. If you aren't sure, use a choke tester (see page 28 and Chapter 7, page 113 for suppliers). If you are not sure, don't put that object in the basket.

The objects listed here are suggestions and starters, you will find more as you become more familiar with this work. Remember, the objects must be clean (wash them in a dishwasher if possible, even if they are new).

Keeping in mind the guidance given in this chapter, start collecting a selection of these:

Objects made of wood and cork	Objects made of metal
• spools	• brass curtain rings
• mug trees	• beakers
• curtain rings	• ash trays or bowls
• egg cups	• a tea strainer or a tea infuser
• different sizes of spoons, scoops and spatulas	• a playground whistle
• baby rattles (wood, cane, gourd)	• napkin rings
• castanets	• a small mouth organ
• napkin rings	• egg cups
• small bowls	• a set of biscuit cutters
• bangles	• different sized whisks
• 'dolly' pegs and clothes pegs	• bulldog paper clips
• boxes	• bells of all sizes
• 'pretend' apples and other fruit	• rings with big stones strung on a string
• big beads on a string	• keyrings
• a darning 'mushroom'	• a bunch of keys
• a small spoon, fork or honey dipper	• a glasses case
• 'pretend' eggs	• a comb
• drawer and door knobs	• a set of spoon measures

- a mustard spoon
- salad servers
- spaghetti measurer
- a wooden foot or back massager
- corks of different sizes
- small musical instruments (rattles, drums, castanets)
- spaghetti measurer
- napkin rings
- bangles
- small boxes
- a lemon squeezer

Objects made of wood and bristle

- a small shoe brush
- a make-up brush
- a nail brush
- a pastry brush
- a nailbrush
- bottle brushes of all sizes
- a mushroom brush
- decorators' paint brushes
- a small hairbrush (wooden handle)
- a bath brush

Natural objects

- fir cones of all sizes
- big shells
- smooth pebbles, big and medium sized
- large chestnuts or walnuts
- big feathers
- big leaves
- corks of different sizes
- a small loofah
- split dried oranges and lemons
- dried gourds
- natural sponges
- marble eggs
- apples
- oranges
- lemons
- pomegranate
- quince

- small mirrors with metal frames
- little tins with lids
- drawer and door knobs
- pet bowls
- bath plug and chain
- a bicycle bell
- lengths of chain of different thicknesses
- spoons of all sizes
- strainers and small sieves
- small tins with screw tops (to fill with rice, dried beans or peas)
- a garlic press
- a small funnel
- egg cups
- a potato masher
- little scoops
- a mustard spoon
- small biscuit tins
- whisks
- tin lids
- a powder compact

Objects made from fabrics, paper, card

- small cardboard boxes
- hair 'scrunchies'
- ribbon
- dressing gown cord
- sequin waste
- small pieces of lace, fur fabric, net, rubber
- lavender bags
- woollen pompom balls
- ribbon, lace and braid
- rag dolls
- fabric bricks or books
- small cloth bags with herbs inside
- bean bags
- a clean flannel
- nail buffers and large emery boards
- cellophane paper, foil, tissue-paper
- a chamois leather or pad

- avocado stones
- a pumice stone

Objects made from cane, raffia, rubber, string, glass, china
- rubber balls
- tennis balls
- a glass lemon squeezer
- rubber door wedges and doorstops
- cane bag handles
- nail buffers and emery boards
- a little empty perfume bottle
- little baskets
- cork, rush or raffia mats and coasters
- string and cane balls
- beads on a string
- a sturdy glass salt pot
- a rubber tap end
- string and cane balls
- a silver survival blanket
- paperweights
- 'snowstorms'

- little fabric gift bags
- small cardboard boxes

Objects made from leather, fur, fabric, paper and wool
- a little leather purse
- a tiny teddy
- a clean flannel
- dressing gown cord
- small pieces of leather, fabric, velvet, lace
- fur fabric
- ribbon, lace, braid
- lavender bags
- tissue-paper, foil, greaseproof paper, cellophane, wrapping paper
- hairbands and 'scrunchies'
- fabric bricks
- fabric books
- bean bags
- fabric and paper gift bags
- small cloth bags with herbs inside

Useful websites for resources

www.consortiumcare.co.uk and www.millwoodeducation.co.uk where you can find starter collections of items. In Chapter 7, see page 110, you will find a longer list of suppliers, all providing materials suitable for heuristic play and treasure baskets. You may want to supplement the list above with some items bought specially, but a successful treasure basket does not need to cost a lot of money!

Using this collection

This basket is ideal for a single sitting baby, or you could sit a baby on each side of the basket as long as this does not cause distress to either baby.

Taking it further/more ideas

This basket is a constant source of interest for all babies. Keep looking for and adding items to maintain their interest, and as you observe them during the sessions, note which items the babies select.

Exploring sensory baskets for babies

As you become more interested in using treasure baskets, you may want to extend your collections by making some themed baskets. These can be:

- sensory baskets, appealing to a single sense, which are also very useful in work with older children with additional needs
- themed baskets with an emphasis on a particular type of object.

These baskets give babies a different sort of experience, and should be used alongside the classic basket to extend their interest, possibly picking up on the observations you make about favorite objects of the babies in your care.

On the following pages you will find guidance on the following baskets:

- Feely fingers – a sensory treasure basket for babies
- Tickle me! – a basket of brushes
- The feel-wood factor – full of a particular range of sensations
- Bath-time! – a bathroom basket to appeal to all the senses.

Name: Feely fingers
Type of collection: A sensory treasure basket for babies
Age group: Sitting babies

Introduction

Rich and stimulating resources and playthings are vital for the brain growth of babies and children. An environment that has plenty of sensory stimulation will ensure that babies can get plenty of this vital input.

The sense of touch is very important to babies and very young children, and it is well developed even at birth. This is why babies use their hands all the time to increase the amount of information they gather about the world, touching and feeling all the time. Touch provides babies with more immediate access to their world than any other sense and has a potent influence over physical growth, emotional development and cognitive potential. Touch is also connected with the immune system, affecting health and physical wellbeing.

A basket full of things selected for their textures will promote exploration of texture, shape, weight, and of coldness, smoothness and pattern. It will give babies a chance to explore all sorts of textured objects. It can provide an engaging alternative to the first treasure basket described on the previous pages.

Container
A shallow basket as described in Chapter 2, see page 29.

What to collect

- fir cones – various sizes and types
- shells – a range of types and sizes
- gourds (either fresh or dried) try to get some with bumpy skins
- big feathers
- a pumice stone
- a loofah
- an apple
- a pomegranate
- a star fruit
- cardboard tubes
- paper (tissue, greaseproof, foil, kitchen roll)
- smooth pebbles
- wooden eggs
- driftwood
- a natural sponge
- corks
- a short length of rope
- a short length of chain with medium links
- some big beads on a string
- a powder puff
- a lemon
- a piece of velvet
- an orange

A useful website for resources
Early Excellence has a collection of natural objects that could be used as a starter for this basket www.earlyexcellence.com

Using this collection
The resource can be used by:
- an individual baby
- a maximum of two babies
- a small group of older children in an adult-led conversation.

Taking it further/more ideas

Add some more objects such as:

- a piece of fur fabric
- a nail brush
- a shaving brush
- a leather purse (if culturally acceptable)

- a triangle
- a fur ball
- a tea strainer
- a raffia coaster

- an avocado pear stone
- a carved wooden bowl

Name: Tickle me!
Type of collection: A treasure basket of brushes for babies
Age group: Sitting babies

Introduction

This is another collection to stimulate the sense of touch. Once you start to look, you will be surprised how many brushes you can collect for this basket! You could also add more than one of each sort – maybe different sizes, colours or weights.

Some, such as make-up brushes, will be soft and tickly, and babies will love to stroke the sensitive skin of their cheeks, hands or feet with them. A bottle-brush is good for waving, a hairbrush stimulates first role play as babies 'brush' their own hair, and older children will often mime the actions as they handle each brush. Everything in a treasure basket will encourage babies to use their fingers, hands and wrists, and brushes are particularly good for practising dexterity, especially the smaller, lighter ones.

Brushing and stroking have a calming effect, so the basket could be offered when a baby has become over stimulated or excited.

Note: Some brushes have long handles or sharp ends, and you should cut these down before adding them to the basket.

Container

A shallow basket as described in Chapter 2, see page 29.

What to collect

- a shaving brush
- a hairbrush (with natural bristles and wooden back)
- a baby's hairbrush
- artists' paintbrushes
- a nailbrush

- a toothbrush
- a pastry brush with wooden handle
- a small dustpan brush (wooden handle)
- small shoe brushes (several)

- a makeup brush
- painting brushes
- mushroom cleaning brush
- a bottle brush
- a washing up brush

A useful website for resources

See www.earlyexcellence.com/u3s/treasure_basket_collections.html for ready-made collections of brushes to put in your own basket.

Using this collection

The resource can be used by:

- an individual baby
- a maximum of two babies
- a small group of older children with an adult.

Taking it further/more ideas

Add some more unusual brushes, such as:

- a metal-backed nail brush
- a stencil brush
- a floor scrubbing brush
- wallpaper brush
- a cat or dog brush (new!)

- a suede cleaning brush
- bottle brushes (several sizes)
- decorating brushes (several sizes)
- a clothes brush

Note: Disinfect the brushes regularly (or put them in the dishwasher) and leave to dry thoroughly before returning to baskets

Name: The feel-wood factor
Type of Collection: A themed treasure basket of wooden objects for babies
Age group: Sitting babies

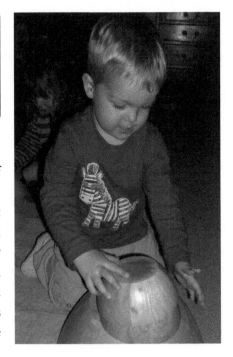

Introduction

This basket is filled with things made of wood.

Wood has two properties that make it very suitable for the components of a themed treasure basket. Firstly, wood gives plenty of sensory information, particularly if you select objects with a range of surfaces and textures. The colours of natural woods are also very valuable as they promote the production of calming endorphins in the brains of babies and young children (and adults too!).

Try to collect a variety of different woods, with a range of grains, patterns and natural colours. Look in your kitchen drawer or utensil holder, or take a walk to collect natural wooden items. Driftwood from the seaside is always a good addition. This will ensure a good variety of textures, shapes and shades to stimulate interest, and you will notice that the natural, neutral appearance of the basket gives a calming contrast to the bright colours of most toys.

Container
A shallow basket as described in Chapter 2, see page 29.

What to collect

- large curly wood shavings
- short lengths of broomstick
- wooden spoons and spatulas
- castanets
- a small boat
- large nuts and seed cases

- coconut shells
- driftwood
- small smooth sticks
- wooden fruit
- small offcuts from a DIY shop or carpenter
- flooring samples
- pieces of bark
- pine cones

- a baby rattle
- chopsticks
- salad servers
- wooden bracelets and bangles
- small carved figures
- cork mats
- corks of different sizes

A useful website for resources
For a large collection of natural materials, suitable for including in different themed baskets, try www.galt-educational.co.uk

Or look in local charity shops for unusual objects made of wood.

Using this collection
The resource can be used by:
- an individual baby
- a maximum of two babies
- a small group of older children in an adult-led exploration.

Taking it further/more ideas

Add some more objects such as:

- curtain rings
- clothes pegs
- wooden boxes
- small bowls
- egg cup
- pastry crimper
- wooden eggs

- wood pencils
- nesting dolls
- small wooden toys
- cotton reels
- wooden spoons
- napkin rings
- salad servers

- wooden beads
- little carvings
- a honey dipper
- a small rolling pin
- 'dolly'pegs

> **Name**: Bath time!
> **Type of collection**: A sensory treasure basket for babies
> **Age group**: Sitting babies

Introduction

There are hundreds of things you could put in a bathroom basket, but they should all be checked for safety and that any liquids, creams and so on are non- allergenic. Try to keep your focus on natural materials – you will find wood, steel, rubber, bristle, cotton, wool, shell, as well as natural perfumes and oils.

For younger children, the basket will be a sensory exploration, so your collection should be aimed at stimulating sight, hearing, touch and smell. Remember the power of texture – babies' experiences of bathrooms should be soft, warm and comforting.

If you can manage it, put babies on a warm, soft surface for all basket work, but particularly with this one, where a fleece blanket, fluffy towel or sheepskin blanket would be ideal.

Container

A shallow basket as described in Chapter 2, see page 29 – you could paint it white and line it with some fleece fabric.

What to collect

- cotton wool balls
- a soft new flannel
- a small towel
- baby powder tin
- baby cream pot (with lid)
- small net bags of pot-pourri

- a toy duck
- large bottle tops
- a toothbrush
- a hairbrush
- a bath brush
- a nail brush
- pumice stone
- a metal beaker

- pieces of cork
- small baskets
- polished stones
- a plug and chain
- a small metal soap holder
- a loofah
- a baby sponge or natural sponge

A useful website for resources

The Wool Company www.thewoolcompany.co.uk sell baby blankets and baby sheep-skins which are perfect for this activity.

Alternatively, you could buy a fleece blanket, or ask parents and carers for spare baby blankets.

Using this collection

The resource can be used by:

- an individual baby
- a maximum of two babies
- a small group of older children.

Taking it further/more ideas

This basket could be used to explore scents as well as taste, touch, sight and hearing. Add some more objects such as:

- empty perfume bottles
- a makeup brush
- a shaving brush
- a stress roller
- shells
- dried flowers

- a wooden boat
- cups and mugs
- a large powder puff
- nail file or emery board

3 Heuristic Play for Older Babies: The Treasure Basket

What are babies like at this stage, and what do they need?

Between ten and fourteen months (some before and some after) babies begin to explore moving around, crawling, creeping, standing (holding on firmly at first), 'cruising' (walking while holding on to furniture), and then taking those long-awaited first steps. Many of their first attempts to walk will lack confidence and many will be short-lived, with stops, starts, rests and sudden returns to the sitting position. All this activity, whether it is hovering on all fours, kneeling by a low stool, lifting head and shoulders off the floor, or pulling themselves up only to sit down with a bump, uses a lot of energy and a huge amount of determination.

Rests between episodes of concentrated movement are common, and during this time, many babies will still return to favourite activities such as a treasure basket, even though they may not stay engaged with it for as long. You will need to use sensitive observation to find out when babies at this stage will welcome a short period of rest from the strenuous exercise associated with moving around. The offer of a session with a familiar basket may be welcomed, or you might consider introducing a new basket, which may contain a selection from your classic basket, or a new collection, selected to stimulate a sense, or drawing together similar objects.

During this time, many (but not all) babies and young children begin to explore and confirm what they are finding out about the world in schema play, repetitive actions and play scenarios such as filling and emptying, wrapping objects up and disclosing them again or looking for things that fit inside each other. Most practitioners will be familiar with this behaviour and some settings plan specifically to respond to the current schemas of individual children, by introducing objects into treasure baskets or other play, which will support the schemas a child is currently exploring. The basket examples in this chapter will give you some ideas for responding to the schemas you observe in your children.

During the period between 12 and 24 months, babies become toddlers, and many will swing violently between independence and moving on, and wanting the comforts of familiar activities and interactions with adults. They want to be babies *and* toddlers, and sometimes feel really torn between the two. Adults feel this tension too! We eagerly await the first step, but realise all too soon that a mobile baby is much more difficult to manage; we want them to be independent but at the same time we still love it when they come back to us for a hug. We should be especially vigilant and responsive to the needs of these emerging toddlers, accepting their move beyond babyhood, while still providing reassurance and familiar activities.

Babies and older children with additional needs will also need continued access to treasure basket collections, to stimulate senses and to encourage the development of physical skills. This group of children may continue to use a treasure basket for many years, as they will need much longer to make sense of what they are experiencing. Children whose behaviour is on the autistic spectrum may welcome a basket of objects particularly selected to appeal to them. Others may be engaged with objects of significance to them personally, and basket collections of objects exactly fulfil this need.

Selecting objects for treasure baskets for older babies and those with additional needs

Many of the principles you should use when selecting or buying objects to include in this next stage of treasure baskets will be the same as those for classic and 'sitting baby' baskets:

- The objects are everyday, easily found objects.
- Everything in the basket is *natural* – no plastic or other man-made materials should be included. If you decide to buy ready-made baskets or collections of contents, check carefully before you buy, as some of these contain man-made objects.

  Note: when putting together objects of reference for children with additional needs, you may need to include some objects that are man-made. As previously advised, you may need to make exceptions in particular cases.

- As babies develop, they may not need to put things in their mouths so often, but as this remains a key way of exploring anything new, you should ensure that the objects are cleaned regularly, either by washing or wiping with a clean damp cloth.

- Fruit or other natural objects are removed and replaced as they deteriorate.
- The objects can't be swallowed. If you aren't sure, use a choke tester (see page 28 and Chapter 7, page 113 for suppliers) or take this piece of advice was given by Elinor Goldschmeid to a worried practitioner: *'If you think an item might be swallowed, put it in your own mouth and see if you could swallow it yourself. You will probably find it is quite impossible.'*

The objects and baskets described in this chapter are very similar to those in Chapter 2, but they are re-organised in ways that make them appropriate to babies' needs at later stages.

Planning for treasure basket sessions

Practitioners working with babies at this crucial stage of development must be aware of the needs of individuals in their group. Some babies will be very happy to take a break from physical exercise to enjoy a more static session. Others may need more support from a familiar adult to engage them in the activity, perhaps selecting one of the items to share, bearing in mind the child's current interests. For example, a child interested in throwing or dropping objects may be engaged by the way a feather falls; the attention of another can be attracted by a tin of dried beans being rattled gently over the basket.

Children with additional needs will often require the attention of an adult throughout the play session. The adult may be guiding the child's hands to objects in the basket, offering things, bringing them into the child's field of vision, or encouraging them to concentrate by talking, chanting, smiling or just joining in the play.

Some ideas for sensory or schema play baskets follow here. Each one is presented in the same format, to allow you to select and incorporate them in your setting.

- Roll along and follow me! – is a basket of things that roll and move along the floor, encouraging babies to follow their movement.
- Listen! – this basket is full of objects that make sounds and noises.
- Feel this – is a basket of textures, appealing to the sense of touch.
- Me and my world – is a personal basket for an individual child with additional needs.

Name: Roll along and follow me!
Type of collection: A rolling schema treasure basket for babies and crawlers.
Age group: Sitting and crawling babies

Introduction

It is now well known that most children at some time develop repetitive behaviours called schemas. These behaviours should not worry parents or practitioners – in schema play, babies and children are practising what they are finding out about the world. Exploring objects that roll, putting things into containers, dropping or throwing things, wrapping things, are all examples of schema play, and some of these can be supported by collections of objects that allow the baby to practise the behaviour or repeated action.

From around nine months many children show an interest in moving themselves and begin to crawl or creep in order to explore the world. At this stage, some children become interested in other things that move too, and a basket of moving, rolling objects may be just the thing to stimulate their interest, and encourage them to crawl.

The items in this collection will spend a lot of time rolling around the floor! Wash or wipe them regularly.

Container

A shallow basket as described in Chapter 2, see page 29.

What to collect

- tennis ball
- pompom wool ball
- rubber ball
- ping pong ball
- small inflatable ball
- decorative cane and string balls
- a ball with a bell inside
- sweet tubes

- quoits of raffia, rubber, wood
- small and larger cardboard rolls and tubes
- serviette rings
- wooden toys with wheels
- curtain rings

Things that roll strangely:
- wooden eggs
- lemons

A useful website for resources

Try www.superstickers.com for small wooden bowls, wooden rings, egg cups, balls and more.

Using this collection

The resource can be used by:

- an individual baby, particularly one interested in rolling and moving objects or in following items as they crawl
- a small group of older children exploring how things move.

Taking it further/more ideas

The rolling collection can be used successfully with older children (from three to seven years old) to explore movement, test and talk about the properties of objects, how they roll and which roll best, sorting rollers and 'non-rollers'. For these children, add some of the objects suggested below, and some objects that don't roll, such as a ruler or a brick.

You could include:

- coins
- apples and oranges
- dried gourds
- round tins and boxes
- nuts

- pebbles and stones
- round beads
- tops from bottles, aerosols, jars
- round corks

- large buttons
- cookie cutters
- pencils and pens
- beakers and cups
- a roll of sticky tape

Name: Listen!
Type of collection: A sensory treasure basket (sense of sound).
Age group: Toddlers and older children

Introduction

Banging and rattling are experiments that babies make with things they can hold or touch – what can I do with this? What sort of sound does it make? Can I bang it on the floor, on the wall, on my leg, on my friend? It is through experiments like this that babies find out about materials and surfaces as well as about the power they have over objects. Rattles are one of the first toys, and babies also love anything they can hold in their hand and shake or rattle. As they bang and rattle objects babies realise their power over inanimate objects, turning them into toys or tools.

Start with natural sound makers and simple home-made shakers. Give the children plenty of time to explore these natural sound-makers by themselves, before making or adding any more formal instruments. This basket can be used indoors or outside, which will give the sounds a different dimension, and where the noise may be less of a problem.

Container

You may want to use a basket with a handle, which makes transporting easier, but it must still have a wide enough top to allow the child to see, reach and select the objects inside. Putting the basket on a hard surface such as a builder's tray or direct on the floor will enhance the sounds the babies make.

What to collect
Natural sound makers:

- paper
- dry leaves
- sandpaper blocks
- small boxes, tubes, tins filled with stones, rice etc
- curtain rings on a string

- key rings
- chain
- wooden baby rattles
- wooden beads on a string
- a small rain stick
- empty tins

- small blocks of wood
- saucepans and spoons
- saucepan lids
- paper or plastic plates
- chopsticks

A useful website for resources
Spotty Green Frog http://www.spottygreenfrog.co.uk has a range of musical instruments for young children.

Using this collection
The resource can be used by:
- toddlers with adult support available
- a small group of older children.

Taking it further/more ideas

When the babies have explored the natural sound-makers, add some simple home-made 'instruments', making them from everyday materials. Children may respond to a short piece of atmospheric music or a simple tape recorder with nursery rhymes and songs.

Home-made instruments:

- containers with stones, pebbles, dry pasta
- wood blocks
- plastic bowl drums
- wood blocks with sandpaper
- drumsticks
- bunches of pegs, keys, bottle tops
- bottle tops nailed on a stick
- kazoos from a comb and paper
- big tin lids

Simple purchased instruments for older toddlers:

- wrist and ankle bells
- wind chimes
- chime bars
- claves or rhythm sticks
- shakers and maracas
- castanets
- small drums
- a guiro
- tambourines without jingles
- bird whistles
- small bongo drums
- click-clacks

> **Name:** Feel this!
> **Type of collection:** A sensory treasure basket (sense of touch).
> **Age group:** Toddlers and older children

Introduction

This 'feely' basket contains all sorts of textures and fabrics to feel. Many children will need to feel the fabrics on their faces, arms and legs as well as their hands. Make sure you include all sorts of fabrics, and in this case, you could include some man-made materials for children to explore and compare with natural materials.

Older children can be encouraged to develop the language of texture through this basket. They associate texture much more with their feelings and experiences than many adults do, so be aware of this as you watch and listen to their responses.

Container
A shallow basket will make the use of this collection easier.

What to collect
Fabrics in this collection may need more frequent washing/cleaning as they will be used as comfort and security objects by some children.
Small pieces are best:

• sequin waste	• cotton	• cotton	• towelling
• a baby sock	• fur fabric	• hand knit fabric	• sandpaper
• silky stuff	• suede	• lurex	• wallpaper
• lace	• satin	• wedding dress fabric	• foam sheet
• gauze or chiffon	• corduroy	• camouflage netting	• hand knit
• fabric with beads, sequins, embroidery	• wool	• lycra	• foil
	• plastic	• velcro	• wood bark
• patent leather	• bubble wrap	• sweatshirt	• bristle brush
• corrugated card	• fleece	• thin foam	• sheepskin
• ribbons of satin, lace, velvet	• fake snakeskin	• elastic	• plastic tray
	• polystyrene sheet	• brocade	• fruit netting
• leaves	• cellophane	• fake grass	• different papers
• floor tiles	• sandpaper	• denim	• egg box
• sacking/hessian	• net curtain		• leather

A useful website for resources
www.dickorydockdesigns.co.uk stock a fantastic range of fabric lengths, including lots of unusual textures.

Using this collection
The resource can be used by:
- one or two of children alone or with an adult.

Taking it further/more ideas
Make a swatch of small pieces of fabrics, so the children can look at it like a book. Use white glue to make patterns on pieces of card (spots, wiggles, lines, letters) or stick sandpaper shapes and letters to wood or thick card.

> **Name:** Me and my world
> **Type of collection:** A personal basket for a child with additional needs.
> **Age group:** Any child with a need to explore familiar objects

Introduction

This is an example of the sort of basket that might appeal to a child who needs reinforcement of experiences. It is just an example, practitioners will need to observe the child as they work with them, talk to parents and other carers and then collect relevant items significant to that child. Try to include items that stimulate every sense.

Note: Check for any allergies before deciding what to include in this basket.

Container

Choose a smaller basket if you need to fit it on a wheelchair or buggy tray. You could line the basket with a piece of appropriate fabric, choosing a colour or design that attracts the child, without distracting from the objects.

A basket for Kim

- a plastic mug with a favourite character
- a model of a superhero character
- a blue flannel
- a fifth birthday card
- a bunch of keys
- a small photo book with family photos
- a soft toy dog
- a dog lead
- a safety mirror
- a bubble bath bottle (empty, but still smelling)
- a lump of 'Aroma dough'
- a yellow toy digger
- a model silver car
- a glasses case with a pair of glasses
- the story of the Gruffalo
- a photo of a baby
- a light-up tambourine

A useful website for resources

Try www.spacekraft.co.uk for all sorts of sensory resources including 'Magic mirrors', light-up tambourine, aromatherapy oils and tactile materials.

Using this collection

This basket should only be used by the named child, with an adult present.

Taking it further/more ideas

Add and remove items as the child's interests change or to maintain focus and attention.

What are children like at this stage, and what do they need?

Toddlers are a breed apart! As they become ever more agile and mobile, they approach the age often called the 'terrible twos' – that almost inflammable combination of confidence and frustration. They are alternately confident learners, pulling, pushing, filling, carrying, tugging, poking, digging; and frustrated, regressive individuals, constantly on the verge of a tantrum or floods of tears.

As babies turn into crawlers and then into toddlers, the 'terrible twos' becomes a very accurate description of their stage of development – and although they still need the presence of familiar adults to return to from time to time, toddlers are beginning to break the ties of attachment to one or two key people, moving into the new world of independence. Self-motivation, self-will and self-confidence increase, resulting in the wriggling struggling mass they can become when their wishes are at variance with those of adults. Two-year-olds have an ability to turn from malleable, friendly, co-operative people to the stiffness of a log or the constituency of jelly in an instant, as they assert their independence. 'No!' becomes the favoured word, 'I can do it!' and 'Let me!' are favourite assertions, and defiance and sudden tantrums become daily behaviours. Adults, parents and practitioners wonder where the docile, smiling, loving child they knew has gone, replaced by this willful, scowling whirlwind of activity.

Once babies can move themselves around, they realise they are free to impact on their own environment, the activities they engage in and the skills they wish to concentrate on. No longer will they accept the toys and playthings we offer them, they want to choose where and what they play with, and they are often deeply involved in exploring schemas, those repeated patterns of behaviour that confirm what they know about the world.

Of course, the child is still the same child as always, it's often just the frustration of new skills that you are seeing. Two-year-olds are independent, yet many don't yet have the communication skills to explain what they want or need, so tantrums or one-word responses result. Toddlers and twos are also using a lot of energy in just moving themselves around. We sometimes underestimate the energy these children put into staying upright, managing crawling, walking, running, riding and relating to other children – in one experiment, an Olympic athlete followed a two-year-old around everywhere they went, copying their behaviour and activity – the athlete was worn out before mid-day, but the toddler was still on the go!

Babies need long periods of time to concentrate on one thing, and practitioners who have watched babies with a treasure basket, will confirm that some babies will concentrate for over 30 minutes on just one or two of the objects offered in a varied basket. Toddlers and twos need just as much time to concentrate, and often find it difficult to stop and start activities with the frequency and speed we expect. Elinor Goldschmeid calls this 'changing gear', which adults find much easier to do than toddlers. In a busy day at home or in a setting, it is much easier to cope with a baby, who we can pick up and carry to another place or for another activity, and our close contact with them as we carry them helps them to manage the gear change more easily. Toddlers get deeply involved in their activities, and often don't get the physical comfort that we naturally give babies. We use language, facial expression, hand holding, and other more distant prompts to give out messages, and often they are not well received, resulting in the typical dawdling or downright defiance.

During this stage of development (once babies become mobile and turn into toddlers) the sedentary basket will no longer engage them in the way it did when they were sitting in one place. The essence of eighteen-months to two-year-olds is that they are learning how to get what they want by going to fetch it. Their bodies and brains keep them on the move and they have very definite agendas, often different from those of the adults who care for them.

As babies grow into toddlers, they also grow out of 'baby toys', needing something more challenging, materials that they can affect, move, organise and arrange. We all know how popular pull-along toys, wheeled prams, carts and barrows, posting boxes, vehicles with people, roadways and train tracks are with children at this stage, and heuristic play also has a place. From the moment a child can move, they have an urge to collect and use real-life objects and natural materials to enhance their play. Some of the ways these 'loose parts' are used include:

- for schema play – exploring by filling, emptying, arranging, covering, wrapping, ordering, dropping, posting
- for imaginative play – representing food, money, shopping, tea-parties, wheelbarrow loads, tickets
- for construction – balancing, building, piling, supporting.

Returning to Elinor Goldschmeid, our mentor in exploring heuristic play, we can find her solution to the problem of providing relevant materials for children at this stage of development. She advises that nurseries and other early years settings consider the place of heuristic play with bags of objects. Her rationale is based on observations of children between eighteen months and two years, and their need for:

- 'Mine' – their own collections of objects. The suggestion is that practitioners meet this need in sheer quantities of objects, so many that there are enough for everyone.
- Movement – this activity encourages movement as children collect and explore the piles of objects on offer.
- Time to explore – the sessions are lengthy, and other activities are not available during heuristic play periods.

During heuristic play sessions, the children are free to explore quantities of resources which are placed on the floor by adults. The next resource available to the children is a range of containers for sorting, organising, arranging, filling and emptying the objects. The final resource is the time allowed for the activity, which is as long as the children need – often between three-quarters of an hour and an hour. This is planned to include involvement of the children in clearing up and putting away the resources.

Heuristic play of this sort is not usually a daily occurrence, nor does it overtake or replace other activities, including adult-initiated and adult-directed activities. This would be unwise and unrealistic! However, in settings where heuristic play is adopted, there are several sessions during the week when children are offered this activity. The practitioners in these settings report that children not only enjoy the sessions, concentrating for substantial amounts of time, but benefit in being calmer and more socially adept.

In this chapter you will find suggestions for using collections and bags of heuristic play materials in focused sessions for toddlers, as described in *People Under Three* (Routledge). In Chapter 5 you will find ways to extend the practice to support child-initiated learning at later stages of development.

The rest of the chapter contains:

- The principles for collecting the objects for heuristic play.
- A list of suitable objects for heuristic play bags for Stage 2 (once babies are on the move) between the ages of around twelve months and three years.
- Ideas for storing the collections of objects.
- Guidance on the organisation and management of the sessions for this stage.
- Some examples of what children do with the materials.

Principles for selecting objects for heuristic play bags

There are several simple principles you should use when selecting or buying objects to include in your heuristic play bags. These are based on the advice from Elinor Goldschmeid in *People Under Three* (Routledge), and have been expanded and amended to apply to the wider age range included in this book:

- Each type of object should be stored in its own strong fabric bag with a wide opening and a drawstring. Some of the objects you collect will not fill the bag, but storage is easier if the bags are all the same size, then any collection of objects can be returned to any bag.

- There should be plenty of objects in each bag.
- The children should have plenty of containers to use with the objects.
- All the objects are everyday, easily-found objects.
- The objects are easy to find in multiple quantities. The objects in a bag can be of slightly different sizes and types, for example, corks or bottle tops of different sizes, but they must be clearly the same object.
- Everything in the bags should be natural – although you may choose to include some man-made materials such as detergent bottle or aerosol tops, or plastic 'corks', try to ensure that the balance overall is of natural materials. Some heuristic play materials on the market contain items made from plastic and other synthetic materials. If you are considering purchasing these contents for your bags, check the range of contents before you buy.
- The objects should be checked regularly and any that become damaged must be removed.
- In any group of toddlers there will be individuals who still put objects in their mouths. You need to check that the objects can't be swallowed by a child. If you aren't sure, use a choke tester from your chemist or the internet (see Chapter 7 for suppliers, page 109) – remember the advice from Elinor Goldschmeid; '... *if in doubt, throw it out!*'

Storage bags for heuristic play sessions

The ideal storage for heuristic play materials is a number of cloth bags, and Elinor Goldschmeid suggests 16 × 20inches (40 × 50cm) is a good size. If you are not good at sewing, you could use pillow-cases, and thread a cord through the top by poking holes in the hem of the open end with scissors and threading a string through. The bags should have a wide opening, so children can help to put away the objects they have been using. The bag can close with a drawstring, a zip, elastic or Velcro, as long as it can open wide for the objects, and has a hanger of some sort. The bags can then hang on hooks in a cupboard or on the wall of the setting. It is best to have the bags hanging, as they will stay neatly out of the way and it will be easy to just lift down the ones you need. Some ready-made bags

are transparent on one side, so you can see the objects inside, but this is not really necessary (see Chapter 7 for a list of suppliers, page 109).

How many bags?

Practitioners sometimes ask how many bags they need to collect for heuristic play. The suggestion is that for a group of eight children, between ten and fifteen bags will provide a basic set, although some settings have collected many more. Only five bags are used in each session, but you do need to have plenty of variety to maintain children's interest and develop their play. However, four bags with 60 items in each could '... *give 13,871,842 different combinations of objects*' People Under Three (Routledge).

What sort of objects?

The objects for heuristic play are many and varied, and the suggestions here are neither compulsory nor an exhaustive list. As with all equipment and resources used with babies and young children, you must decide yourself which objects you will put in your heuristic play bags. The general advice is 'if you aren't happy with or can't get enough of any object on the list, don't collect it'!

Receptacles for heuristic play sessions

Children will need tins, bowls and boxes in their work with the objects. They will want to fill, empty, arrange, transport, pile and dump the objects, so you will need plenty of good strong containers in a variety of sizes. Elinor Goldschmeid suggests offering at least three containers for each child, so you will need about 25–30 for a group of eight children. These could be:

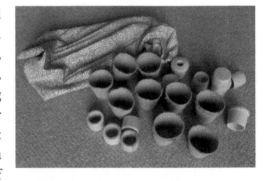

- Empty food tins, washed and with any sharp bits smoothed out. Use the handle of a tablespoon to press the sharp edges flat, and cover the edges with duct tape if you want to be extra careful. Baby food formula tins or others that have plastic tops often have smoother edges than those opened with a tin opener.

- Metal bowls – try Asian shops for stainless steel bowls in various sizes, or pet shops for metal pet bowls (see Chapter 7 for suppliers, page 109).
- You can also include other containers such as trays, small boxes (with or without lids), patty tins, gift bags, egg boxes.

Objects for heuristic play bags

The following list of over 30 different objects has been constructed for practitioners who want to start collecting, and as a checklist for those of you with more experience. You will certainly be able to add to it.

Keeping the above principles in mind, start by looking for some of these (see suppliers in Chapter 7, page 109).

You may already have these or be able to collect them yourself, or have them donated by asking colleagues, friends and the parents of the children in your setting:

- small bags and boxes with and without lids
- empty food cans (with sharp bits smoothed out)
- cardboard cylinders of all shapes and sizes (such as those in the middle of kitchen roll, cling film or foil)
- lengths of ribbon, string, tape, lace
- wood off-cuts (sanded smooth)
- wooden doorknobs
- small padlocks
- coconut shells
- old keys
- rubber balls
- tennis balls

- large shells
- bottle corks
- pine cones
- metal tops from bottles and jars
- wooden or metal bangles
- hair 'scrunchies'
- conkers, large nuts and seed shells
- large seeds such as conkers or chestnuts
- woollen pompoms
- rubber doorstops
- rubber door wedges
- hosiery yarn cones
- cotton reels

You will probably need to buy these:

- curtain rings (wooden or metal)
- 'dolly' clothes pegs and 'clip' clothes pegs – in separate bags
- large and small corks
- cork balls
- wooden eggs

- wooden shapes
- large wooden beads
- dried oranges and lemons
- lengths of ribbon of all sorts and widths, and lengths of lace (market stalls often have ends of rolls at bargain prices)

- rubber door stops (round and wedge shaped)
- varied lengths of chain – fine and medium sized links
- wooden balls
- large bone buttons
- hosiery yarn cones
- small pieces of fabric of all sorts
- wooden door and drawer knobs
- wooden dice

Containers:

- wooden bowls
- metal bowls
- boxes
- bangle and ring holders
- mug trees
- cardboard tubes

Planning and organising the sessions

How do I start?

- Find or make some drawstring cloth bags at least 40 × 50cm in size. The drawstring allows the children to help with the clearing up, which is an essential part of the activity. You need at least 12 bags before you start, so you have a good choice for each session. Some settings put the name or a picture of the contents on each bag, but this is not essential, as all the objects are emptied out of each bag during the session, and may not end up back in the same bag.
- Create as many different collections of objects as you can and put each collection in its own bag. Each bag should contain only one type of object, and there should be between 30 and 60 items in each bag. Suggestions for objects, (including items to buy in bulk) are included on the previous pages and in Chapter 7.

How should I store the collections of objects?

- The objects should be stored in their drawstring bags, on hooks in any convenient place. Ideally each bag should have its own hook, but this may not be possible – particularly if you are good at finding different items! (Remember Elinor Goldschmeid found a setting with 36 different bags!)

What do I need for a session?

- At least 12 bags of objects (you will be using four or five for each session).

- Containers (at least 20 for a group of 8 children).
- A clear space on the floor, with as few distractions as possible.

How many children can be involved at a time?

- Eight children is a good number.

Preparation

- Ensure the space is clear and free of distractions. Other activities should stop during sessions for children at this stage.
- Select four or five bags of objects, making sure there is good variety. You will be rotating the bags in future sessions, mixing them to get endless combinations.

How do I start the activity?

- Tip the contents in heaps, spaced out across the floor.
- Place the containers in groups.
- Put the bags near your chair.
- Add children!

What may happen?

- The children will probably not need any encouragement to get involved, if they start immediately, you need to do no more, except stay and watch what they do.
- If individual children don't get involved immediately, you may need to sit near them and model the play, selecting objects yourself and exploring them, offering the child an object, or putting a container between you and adding an object to it, inviting them to join in.
- If any child appears to be distressed sit with them and talk about what the other children are doing as you watch together – this may be enough to start them off.

What do I do next?

- Your main role in this activity is to prepare the resources and plan enough time for the children to play undisturbed.

- Once the children have started playing, your job is to observe, only intervening if individuals become distressed or if there are disputes over resources or space. Experienced practitioners report that disputes are rare, particularly when there are plenty of items in the bags and space to play.

Tips for clearing up

- Make sure you leave enough time for clearing up, which is a vital part of the activity. When it is time to stop, encourage the children to bring the objects to you and put them in the correct bags. When you first start this activity, it may take more adult support than later, when the children are used to the process.

What children might do with the resources:

Abbie selects a metal tin and a handful of metal bottle tops. She sits down and drops the tops one by one into the tin. Then she tips the tops out and repeats the activity.

Ben squats down by a pile of dolly pegs. He looks round for a container and finds a tin. He carefully places each of the dolly pegs on the edge of the tin, moving the tin round until he has completely filled the edge with pegs. He smiles as he finishes and looks up at the adult, who smiles back.

Molly carefully takes the lid off a small oblong box. She has filled it with corks, lined up next to each other and nearly exactly filling the box. She finds a small piece of wood and fits it in the box so the box is completely full.

Morgan fills a bowl to the brim with lengths of chain. He then gets another bowl and tips this upside down over the first bowl. He peeps under the bowl to see the contents, then carefully places a block of wood on the top.

Saraj sits with his legs stuck out and balances lengths of string along the length of them. He finds this too difficult, and rearranges them across his legs. Then he decides to collect something else. So he carefully takes the strings off and lays them on the floor, gets up and collects some big shells. He sits down again, lays the strings on his legs, and puts a big shell on each knee.

Mina puts a ping-pong ball in a metal bowl. She swishes the ball round and listens carefully to the sound it makes. She takes the ball out and puts a stone in the bowl, repeating the action.

As you can see from these examples, children respond in very different ways to the resources you offer, exploring, arranging and rearranging as they play with concentration. The unhurried time scale is essential and the abundance of materials limits disputes. The constant presence of an appreciative adult gives a clear message about the importance of this activity.

5

Heuristic Play for Older Children: The Theory of 'Loose Parts'

What is the theory of 'loose parts'?

The theory was first aired in the 1970s by an architect called Simon Nicholson, when he proposed that:

> 'The simple facts are these: There is no evidence, except in special cases of mental disability, that some young babies are born creative and inventive, and others not.
>
> There is evidence that all children love to interact with variables, such as materials and shapes; smells and other physical phenomena, such as electricity, magnetism and gravity; media such as gases and fluids; sounds, music, motion; chemical interactions, cooking and fire; and other humans, and animals, plants, words, concepts and ideas. With all these things all children love to play, experiment, discover and invent and have fun.
>
> All these things have one thing in common, which is variables or 'loose parts'. The theory of loose parts says, quite simply, the following:
>
> In any environment, both the degree of inventiveness and creativity, and the possibility of discovery, are directly proportional to the number and kind of variables in it.'
>
> Nicholson, S., 'How Not To Cheat Children: The theory of loose parts'
> *Landscape Architecture*, v62 (1971)

He was very clear that if we want children to be inventive and creative, we must offer them a wide range of these 'loose parts', referred to earlier in this book as heuristic play materials, which are in abundance on beaches and in woods, but scarce in many school classrooms or playgrounds. These 'loose parts' are not as available to children in the 21ˢᵗ Century when, unlike their parents and grandparents, they spend more time in school, their parents are reluctant to let them roam freely in fields and parks after school, and families spend much of their free time either shopping or watching a screen (an object with no loose parts!). Simon Nicholson, and those who have followed his advice, encouraged teachers, parents and those who build playgrounds and museums for children to make children's places (both indoors and outside) full of the loose parts that children of previous generations enjoyed.

What are children like at this stage, and what do they need?

Between three and seven years of age (often referred to as the later part of the early years), children respond best to gradual changes in both the resources and the organisation of learning. Where this understanding of child development has been taken seriously, the curriculum for under threes and the curriculum for three to seven-year-olds is strongly linked, and the environment only changes very gradually from the baby room to the classroom. Resources, organisation, access to the outdoor environment, and an emphasis on play and exploration are common across the age range, within which the crucial role of the adult is the key. These adults, knowledgeable in child development, manage the curriculum to meet the needs of the children, starting from the child, not the curriculum guidance, and creating a space where those magical 'loose parts' can support, extend and enhance a declared curriculum.

Just because children have reached the age of three (the age of entry to government funded nursery schools or classes in much of Europe) they do not magically become just 'pupils', learning only what the teacher presents them with. One dictionary definition of 'pupil' is – *a person, usually young, who is learning under the close supervision of a teacher at school*, and it is heartening to hear the most often used word to describe this age is 'children' not 'pupils'. Moreover, in many countries, including Wales and Scotland, the curriculum now follows the model used in Scandinavian countries by legislating that the early years curriculum should cover the ages from birth to around seven:

> '... *research evidence shows that children do not begin to benefit from extensive formal teaching until about the age of six or seven.'*
> ESTYN, Inspection in Wales (2011)

Of course, the provision for seven-year-olds will differ significantly from that for babies and even from that for three-year-olds, but the principles should be the same:

- Much of the play should be initiated by the child.
- Children should have time to explore and discover for themselves, and long periods of uninterrupted time will result in more enjoyable and effective learning.
- As children master skills (emotional, social, intellectual and physical), they need to practise these repeatedly in their play, alone and with friends. The outside environment is just as important as the indoor environment to children, and should be organised and resourced with just as much care.
- The adults should observe children regularly and carefully, intervening sensitively as a genuine partner in thinking and learning.
- The resources offered should provide a good balance of open-ended materials (loose parts) and resources with more structure and limited uses.

As children move through nursery and into the early years of school, they will continue to grow in confidence and independence. However, their confidence and creativity will only become secure if they have the support of sensitive adults who understand their need for exploratory play to confirm their growing knowledge of the world and of their own abilities.

A feature of the play of these older children is that they enjoy working with friends on projects, some of which take days to complete, needing an abundance of space and time. It is also clear that the more they become interested in the world, the more they will respond to open-ended materials, and that these will not only include those previously explored through treasure baskets and heuristic play bags, but larger, more complex materials such as tyres, planks and ropes. These items will be welcomed as they are presented on suitable scales for both indoor and outdoor play, as construction, exploration and invention should be able to take place with the same sense of excitement and creativity in both situations. This is the reason for providing an extended list of 'loose parts' materials in this chapter of the book, so you can consider your current provision and how this might be extended to make best use of your own spaces.

One of the reasons given for restricting this sort of provision as children get older is that there is not enough space for extended and complex play, particularly out of doors. You should not accept this restriction, and this is why – every time an adult demonstrates or teaches a new skill or talks with children about a new piece of knowledge, the children need to practise the skill until it is fixed in their brains. This process is called myelination, and is the way we all turn the 'soft wiring' of new experiences into the 'hard wiring' of permanent skills and abilities. This is why young children enjoy the same bedtime story over and over again, insist on walking round the park in the same direction on each visit, practise new words such as 'tyranno-saurus' repeatedly.

When babies get involved in myelination, they repeat gestures and movements again and again (we call these behaviours *schemas*). When older children are myelinating their learning, they will also certainly be revisiting lots of different jigsaw pieces of experiences, all at the same time, or in subtle sequences. Careful and experienced observers will be able to spot these – the child who chooses the same activity day after day, building bricks, playing trains or playing out their home lives in the house corner; the child who needs the tactile experiences of sand and water and is distraught if there is no room for them; even the child who appears to be flitting about from activity to activity may just be fruitlessly looking for the activity that will meet all their myelination demands, only to find that such an activity doesn't exist, or isn't available on that day. One thing about myelination is that we cannot be sure what each child needs, and they may not know either until they see it (or invent it).

Providing 'loose parts' and heuristic play materials has a much better chance of meeting the many needs of a group of children, as the children can then select the materials that best fit their interests, often in combination with more traditional educational toys and games. Watch the child carefully selecting the smaller stones from a bucket to fill the wagons of the train set; or one fetching water from the sink to make real 'tea' to pour into the cups. Look at the group adding to a static climbing frame with planks, ropes, fabrics and tyres to transform it into a superhero castle, or the concentration of children collecting leaves, grass and sticks to make a habitat for a visiting snail.

Loose parts work is never tidy! Embrace the method and you will need:

- patience – to wait until children have finished, or make space for unfinished projects

- persistence – to convince colleagues and parents that 'loose parts' play really has a purpose and benefit
- flexibility – to adapt your programme to the changing needs and interests of individuals and groups.

But the benefits far outweigh the difficulties. Settings and schools where children are encouraged to extend their learning in a culture of flexible, supportive and creative environments *do* outstrip the learning of children in more restrictive environments. They *don't* lose momentum when assessed or tested, in fact they excell, particularly in those vital skills of creativity, critical thinking, problem solving and social maturity, which will create a firm foundation for future learning.

Physically, emotionally and intellectually, individual children will vary greatly in their ability to become independent and creative learners. Some will be less mature or less confident, and may need more support from adults to expand their concentration and really get involved in a more creative provision. Others may be restricted by their experiences outside nursery or school, in homes where inventiveness and creativity are not encouraged, and these children may find it more difficult to relax into a more fluid situation. Yet other children will have behavioural or learning difficulties that slow down or otherwise restrict their development, and these children will need more support, and perhaps more experience of earlier stages of the process, including the continued use of treasure baskets, sensory collections, personal objects of reference, or heuristic play bags.

It has been said by child development experts that children with learning difficulties may just need more repetitions of activities than children of average ability, and those with behavioural difficulties will probably be suffering from the effects of stress hormones in their bodies and brains, which prevent them from concentrating as well as others. For both of these groups, the myelination process simply takes longer, and in some *much* longer, and affects all sorts of learning from communication, physical skills, and cognitive development. The way to support these children is through sensitive observation, noting their current interests and matching your expectations to the stage of their development, not just their age.

Frustration can often result from our (or the children's own) unreasonable expectations of their ability, and this can emerge in many children, not just those with learning difficulties. Sometimes children will become frustrated, either by:

- The lack of time to complete long projects or the need to put away materials according to a timetable.
- Their inability to create the things they imagine (their 'Grand Designs'), and the most able children are often perfectionists!
- Their frustration with the inadequacy of the resources we offer them (for example glue that doesn't stick, scissors that don't cut, not enough of the objects they need).
- Conflicts of purpose between children, when each of them has a clear idea of what they want to do. This can be a problem at any age, and requires us to be vigilant and to teach the skills of negotiation and consensus.

The inclusion of 'loose parts' play is so valuable, and essential if we are going to provide children with the resilience, sociability and creativity they will need to be successful in this uncertain world, where creativity and problem solving will be key skills for success.

Where does 'loose parts' play fit in the curriculum?

At the end of this chapter (see page 81) you will find some suggestions for 'loose parts' play linked to topics and themes you may be undertaking with your group. Children will be able to use these collections of themed resources to expand their learning about areas that you have decided to explore in detail, either as part of your scheme, or as centres of interest as you pick up on and follow the interests of individuals and groups.

You can also use the method and the collections of materials to follow up on visits, walks and the visitors who you have invited to meet the children. You will also find some of these later in this chapter (see page 86).

However, the major contribution that 'loose parts' make to children's learning is in providing flexible, open-ended resources that can be used for a variety of purposes, including revisiting significant experiences that you have offered the children and which they follow up in child-initiated sessions. Basket collections of stimuli, combined with a setting or classroom where 'loose parts' play is valued, will enable children to take what they need from stories, and other experiences.

They might perhaps use small-world figures to explore an environment built from tubes, guttering and drainpipes; or recreate a recent walk by combining leaves and other natural materials collected in the park to make a picture in the sand. Similarly, they might experiment with planks and other large materials to recreate a fire station after a visit or to make a trap for a Gruffalo.

Is 'loose parts' play the same as technology with found and recycled materials?

This sort of play, particularly when children become absorbed in it indoors, will overlap with many other areas of your provision – technology, science, construction, art, drama and role play, exploration of places and the past – and more. The difference is that children should be encouraged to combine materials in the ways that suit their purposes, usually in temporary creations, where the *process* of designing, problem solving, building, making, constructing and discussing is far more important than any *product* that may emerge at the end. The constructions emerging from 'loose parts' or heuristic play may last for several days, but their essence is that they are 'works in progress', changing day by day, and with their usefulness exhausted over time, when the resources are often returned by the children to be re-used by others.

The area often called 'the making area' in nurseries and classrooms is an area where children exclusively practise their manipulative and craft skills – cutting, sticking, balancing, painting – usually following suggestion by adults of what they should make, and coming up with something that only approximates what they imagined at the start. Some children find this activity rewarding and gravitate towards it regularly. Others find the activity frustrating and disappointing, and really want to use the materials in a much less permanent way.

Incorporating 'loose parts' materials and reducing the emphasis on product can free children from some of the frustrations of 'making', and making the resources much more freely used. This might involve taking yogurt pots outside to use in the digging area; fetching a cardboard tube to use as a telescope at the top of the climbing frame, or using a remnant of fabric to wrap a soft toy. These examples show how freeing children from the expectation that resources are only used in one area of the room will release creativity and enable real thinking.

Three to seven-year-olds are making huge leaps in their learning, but they still need the security of familiar resources, the freedom to use them in the ways they invent, and permission to be imaginative as they explore the experiences we offer them, and convert them into learning.

And of course the adults are the key to success in this philosophy. They need to be confident, knowledgeable risk takers, and that is not always easy, particularly in these days of pressure and sudden change. However, everything the brain researchers tell us says that if we offer children significant experiences, teach them the skills they need to do what they want to do, and then give them plenty of time to replay and practise these in free play with real-life objects, we will help them to become learners for life.

In the rest of this chapter you will find:

- The principles for collecting the objects for 'loose parts' play.
- A list of suitable objects for play for Stages 3 and 4, between the ages of around three and seven years.
- Ideas for storing the collections of objects.
- Guidance on the organisation and management of the sessions for this stage, both indoors and outside.
- Themed collections to support and enhance 'loose parts' play
- Examples of what children might do with the materials.

Principles for selecting objects for 'loose parts' play

There are several simple principles you should use when selecting or buying objects to include in your 'loose parts' play. These are based on recent research into child development, the writings of those exploring 'loose parts' and flexible play, and the principles previously offered for heuristic play at earlier stages:

- Most of the objects will be everyday, easily-found objects, but your collection can now include some more unusual items, and these may need imaginative sourcing. Practitioners and teachers should use their professional judgement as well as their initiative in locating stimulating resources appropriate to the children (see Chapter 7, page 109, for further resources).

- Natural resources should predominate, but adults may locate, or be offered man-made objects that enhance 'loose parts' play.
- The resources should be available both *indoors* and *outside*. The two different parts of your setting may need items on different scales, but the variety and range should be just as inviting in both, and movement between them should be encouraged.
- There should be sufficient quantities for purposeful play without conflict. Small items in particular will be popular and need to be plentiful. The smaller items will also be more likely to get lost, so you'll need to replenish them more often.
- The resources should be stored to enable *easy access* by the children. They should be available at all times when children are initiating their own play.
- Resources should be of good quality, in good condition and regularly checked by adults. Any that become damaged, splintered or dangerous must be removed.
- The resources should reflect and extend the interests of the children.
- Some children may still put objects in their mouths. You should check for possible choking hazards by using a choke tester (see page 28 and Chapter 7, page 113, for suppliers), particularly if you are working with children with additional needs who may habitually 'mouth' objects.

Storing 'loose parts' materials

Out of doors

Resources for outdoor play may need to be put away at the end of the day, and this may dictate the sort of storage you can arrange. Ideally, even if you need to store 'loose parts' in a shed or other closed area, try to make sure the children can get them out by themselves. If you have wheeled toys in the same shed, keep these in the middle, let the children wheel them out first, then you can hang or store the 'loose parts' in bags or boxes against the shed walls, where they children can collect them for their play. Smaller objects can be stored in wheeled trolleys or bags hung from hooks.

Larger weatherproof items such as guttering, tyres, planks, bowls, buckets and crates can be stored outside, but you will need to provide some cover for such things as tubes from carpet rolls, fabrics, and large cardboard boxes.

Indoors

The resources for 'loose parts' play indoors will probably be smaller in scale, but of course they will have to compete for space in your room alongside all your other equipment. Units with clear plastic drawers, wire trolleys and plastic crates, plastic bags on hooks, sorting trays, tins, boxes and trays will all help you to present the materials so that children can find them and help themselves. In this way, the children 'select the materials they need for the task' and decide where, how and what they will do to explore either their own ideas or provocations and challenges presented by adults.

How many resources?

There needs to be 'enough'! But of course, you will need to decide what that means for you. However, if there are insufficient materials then frustration and conflict may well result as children hoard the materials available. In most settings for children across this age group, a wide variety of activities are going on at any one time, some led by adults and some chosen by children, and this organisation can relieve some of the pressure on resources. However, you do need to keep in mind that 'loose parts' play needs plenty of 'stuff' and that means lots of objects of different types and sizes, containers and joining materials!

   As with all heuristic and 'loose parts' play, the general advice is 'if you aren't happy with or can't get enough of any object on the list, don't collect it'!

Objects for 'loose parts' play objects for older children

The following list is separated into three – small, medium sized and larger items. Some are the same items that have been suggested for younger children, others are new. You will certainly be able to add to this list.

Small resources

- small bags and boxes with and without lids
- cardboard cylinders of all shapes and sizes (such as those in the middle of kitchen roll, cling film or foil)
- lengths of ribbon, string, tape, lace
- metal tops from bottles and jars
- old CDs and DVDs
- plastic, wooden, metal bangles
- hair 'scrunchies'
- charity wristbands

- wood off-cuts (sanded smooth)
- small padlocks
- coconut shells
- old keys
- large shells
- polished stones
- gravel
- bottle corks
- pine cones
- bark, moss
- nuts and bolts
- charity shop beads
- keyrings
- old watches and clocks
- ball pool balls
- paper clips, paper fasteners
- leather shoelaces
- real and fake moss
- hair rollers of different sizes
- ping-pong balls
- 'ball pool' balls
- large and small corks
- large wooden beads
- lengths of ribbon of all sorts and widths, and lengths of lace
- small pieces of fabric of all sorts
- buttons of all sorts and sizes
- small plastic bottles with lids
- plastic food trays
- lolly sticks
- balsa wood

- conkers, large nuts such as chestnuts, and seed shells
- dried peas and beans, rice,
- glass 'beads'
- cotton reels
- hosiery yarn cones
- curtain rings (wooden or metal)
- feathers
- leaves
- labels of all sorts
- raffia
- marbles
- sequins
- coins
- washers
- sticks and chopsticks
- paper and plastic straws
- small spoons
- wrapping paper
- foil
- sweet and snack tubes
- And for joining and fixing
- clothes pegs, bulldog clips
- duct tape
- masking tape
- cable ties
- string, wool, tape, braid, laces
- 'dolly' clothes pegs and 'clip' clothes pegs – in separate bags
- pipe cleaners
- paper fasteners, treasury tags
- elastic bands

Medium-sized resources

- baskets
- bowls
- buckets and spades
- bags of all sorts
- plastic plant pots (all sizes

- plant trays and saucers
- builders trays
- plastic storage boxes
- hose and plastic tubing
- bike tyres and inner tubes

- paper and plastic cups and plates
- small slices of log
- larger pieces of fabric and sheets
- carpet samples and tiles
- rugs and cushions

- bike wheels
- umbrella frames
- torches
- cameras
- empty food cans (with sharp bits smoothed out)

Larger resources

- logs
- planks
- rope
- crates
- cardboard boxes and packing material
- guttering and drainpipes
- garden trugs
- barrows and carts
- shower curtains
- old sheets and blankets

- bubble wrap
- a tarpaulin
- big stones and rocks
- pulleys
- car and tractor tyres
- cable reels
- free standing A-frames and ladders
- tree trunk slices
- netting
- canes

Some ideas for storage

For smaller items:
- plastic sorting trays (for very small items)
- hobby boxes with sections or drawers
- plastic food trays
- small buckets and baskets
- yogurt pots with lids
- bun tins

For larger items:
- plastic boxes
- vegetable baskets (stacking or separate)
- sets of drawers (labelled or ideally clear plastic)
- plastic baskets from 'Pound' shops
- baskets with wheels
- stacking boxes
- shopping baskets
- buckets
- washing up baskets
- washing up bowls
- baby baths
- fabric bags
- plastic garden trugs (try ebay for bargain packs of three)
- collapsible picnic baskets

Planning and organising 'loose parts' play

How do I start?

If heuristic play is a new idea for you, the first thing is to make sure that you, your managers and everyone in your team understands what you are doing, and is happy with the way you are changing things. Taking other people with you may involve you in discussions and possibly even disagreements, and you may have to go more slowly than you might wish in order to get everyone on board. You should also make sure that parents understand why things are changing and what the benefits will be.

'Loose parts' play is a natural extension of child-initiated learning, so the materials offered to the children can be added bit by bit to the resources you already have. You will need to introduce the materials as you add them, but make sure you ask the children what they think they could be used for – if you tell them, they may not use their own creative thinking in the same way.

Explain that the materials belong to everyone and that children should return what they have used when they have finished playing, and of course, you may need to ask the children how they think everyone should take care of the new resources so they don't get lost or damaged. This way of involving the children follows naturally from heuristic play sessions for younger children, where clearing up is a planned part of the session. Clear labelling and accessible storage underpins the provision.

You could start by arranging some child-initiated sessions for everyone at once, so all the adults are available to respond to needs and act as 'play partners', being careful not to dominate the play. During these whole group sessions it would be easier to suggest or remind children of the new resources. You will need to ensure that there are plenty of the new resources for everyone, as they will be very popular!

Another way is to introduce the resources a bit at a time into existing continuous provision, making sure that an adult is present to support and suggest, perhaps even introducing each new resource to the children at the start of a session, showing them where to find each type of object and encouraging the children to collect what they need. This is a more natural way to introduce the new resources, and you can continue to add more week by week as you locate or acquire them.

Whichever method you use to introduce 'loose parts', the children need to see that you are interested in their play and the way they are using the new objects. One way is to be with them as they play, genuinely being an equal, sharing the thinking and enjoyment with them. Another way is to make sure that you feed back to the whole group on these independent and creative activities, either by asking children to show or talk about what they have been doing. Photos are great, particularly with the more ephemeral parts of 'loose parts' play. This may be a point where adults can help, by recording in notes, photo series or video.

Tips for clearing up

Make sure you leave enough time for clearing up, which is a vital part of any activity. Give children a warning, so they have time to bring their play to a natural close and clear up without rushing (or nagging). Remind children that if they haven't finished their game, they can either take some photos to remind themselves, or keep the creations they have made. Of course, this presumes you have space and that your cleaners have been briefed! Making some space for unfinished creations, and the use of a digital camera really pays off.

What children might do with the 'loose parts' resources:

Tony, Marta, David and Dana roll the log slices to the fence and make a half ring of them. It takes some time and a great deal of effort. They sit on the logs and start to tell a complicated story where one child at a time stands up in the middle of the semicircle and sings a song.

Paul has filled his pockets with plastic, multicoloured 'ball pool' balls. He climbs to the top of the plastic slide in the play area. He calls his friend Marrin to stand at the bottom of the slide. They spend half an hour rolling the balls down the slide to each other, taking turns. When Abbie (one of the teachers) asks them what they have found out, they say the blue balls go faster!

Paran has collected together some of the objects the class found when they went for a walk yesterday. He has moss, conkers, bark, leaves and stones. He takes a plant saucer and scoops up some sand, wetting it a bit under the tap. Then he carefully arranges the natural objects in the sand and takes a photo of his work, which he shows to the rest of the children and to his mum when she fetches him. His project inspires other children to make natural gardens using the objects from the walk, adding dough, shiny paper, small world figures and animals. They ask an adult to help them look up miniature gardens on the internet.

Ellie finds some empty plastic plant pots and some straws. She lines the pots up, upside down on a table and puts a straw into a hole in each pot. Then she fetches some paper and a glue stick and makes a flag for each straw. When Mandeep comes over, she says 'It's my sandcastles'.

Sunny finds a cardboard box. He carefully cuts it and flattens it out. He experiments with standing the card sheet up, bending it so it stands up like a screen. Then he asks an adult to help him cut a window in the card. He goes round behind the screen of card and says 'I'm on TV!' Later he and some friends put on a show using Sunny's TV screen.

The class has been given 200 old CDs. They discuss with the adults how they could use them. Three children spend most of the morning making a path of CDs in and out of the furniture, all round the nursery. They use all the CDs.

Later the same day, two children make spinners by putting pencils through the holes in the CDs. This starts a real interest and lots of experiment in what else makes a good spinner.

A group of children have started to make a den under the climbing frame in the playground. They fix a shower curtain round the bottom layer with duct tape and cable ties. Then they climb up the frame and attach a bucket with a length of rope, experimenting to find the best way to pull it up. They spend the rest of the session raising and lowering objects in the bucket.

Keely and Kerry, inseparable friends have found a collection of foreign coins at Keely's house. They have brought these to school and start to make a coin museum. They make a cabinet for the coins from two strong gift boxes, adding shelves for their coin collection. They research their coins using the internet, and make a label for each one, saying where it came from and its date. They set up a ticket system for entry to the museum, asking Paul to be on the ticket desk as they show people around. Over the next few days the children bring other coins for the collection, which expands to take these new exhibits. The children ask if they can go to the local museum to see if there are any coins there.

As you can see from these examples, children respond in very different ways to 'loose parts' resources collected from everywhere, including their own homes. They show interest and enthusiasm in their own projects, involving others, planning, undertaking preparation, collecting materials and researching their interests. The continued presence of an appreciative adult, and opportunities to feed back to others enhance the experiences.

Using collections of materials to enhance 'loose parts' play

There are many ways to enhance child-initiated 'loose parts' play, and one of these could be by offering collections of materials to meet specific purposes or interests. These baskets can be used on their own, or with 'loose parts' materials to explore concepts, skills and new knowledge. This sort of collection might be:

- A themed basket of objects to stimulate the senses and encourage discussion and exploration.
- A basket of objects to support a current theme or topic of interest to the children.
- A basket to promote recall and retelling of stories and poems.
- A collection to promote thinking and problem solving.

On the pages that follow you will find examples of these collections. They are intended as examples – you will need to observe the children in your group and decide how you might use this type of heuristic resource. Of course, they can be used instead of 'loose parts', but are more successful if they are embedded in practice where adults observe children's play and promote this by selecting and offering additional stimuli, which the children can add to their day-to-day play.

The rest of this chapter contains examples of themed objects for discussion, free play, and thinking skills. They are:

- Chink! Chink! Clink! Clink! – a metal basket for exploring the sense of sound and the texture of metal.

- Lovely light and colour – a basket collection for exploring light and colour.
- Put it in – a collection for exploring containers.
- Where have we been? – collections with a focus on the places children have visited.
- Our visitor – collections with a focus on the visitors who have met the children.
- 'Oh we do like to be beside the seaside!' – a detailed example of a themed collection to inspire topic work, or encourage recall of a visit.
- Before me – a collection of historical objects to encourage exploration of the past.
- Light and heavy – a collection to encourage exploration of mass and weight.
- Will it float? – a collection to encourage exploration of floating and sinking.
- Sticky magnets! – another themed collection with a science focus.
- Sort the sound – games with phonics; phonic treasure baskets.
- What's the difference? – a collection to encourage thinking.
- Shapes without names – another basket to support thinking and creativity.

Name: Chink! Chink! Clink! Clink!
Type of collection: A collection for exploring metals and the sense of sound
Age group: Three to seven-year-olds

Introduction

This metal basket is noisy, so be prepared for this. It is a collection of all the metal objects from a traditional treasure basket, and more! For younger children, you might make a smaller collection, adding more as they become familiar with the properties of the metals.

Exploring sounds, textures, reflections, and movement of these objects will fascinate children of all ages. They will be intrigued by the crash, tinkle, clang and clatter as they explore and move the objects. The coldness of metal is another feature as the sense of touch is stimulated.

Older children will be able to sort and classify the items into different

purposes, types, or even different metals. You could also use the items to explore magnetism. Hang a wind chime near the area where the children will be working.

Container

A shallow basket, as described in Chapter 2, see page 29. You could spray the basket with silver or gold paint. If you don't mind the noise, you could use a big metal bowl.

What to collect

- spoons and forks of various sizes and shapes
- keys in bunches on strings and rings
- keyrings strung together
- a plug with a chain
- small whisks
- a tea straine
- a metal cruet set
- a metal toy car
- tin lids
- small tins

- bulldog clips
- paper clips
- nuts and bolts
- big washers
- coins
- small bells
- a bike bell
- costume jewellery
- mirror with metal frame
- a metal ash tray
- small baking tins
- a garlic press
- lengths of chain
- an enamel mug

- metal kitchen implements

Some musical instruments:
- a triangle
- bells
- a small cymbal
- a chime bar
- wind chimes
- a harmonica

A useful website for resources

http://www.tts-group.co.uk sell a ten-piece cooking set. Or you could try charity shops or camping shops.

Using this collection

The resource can be used:

- for exploration in a small group, or with an adult.

Taking it further/more ideas

Add some more unusual objects:

- a dog chain
- a whistle
- a lemon press
- a bunch of bells
- a metal doorknob

- brass curtain rings
- a metal funnel
- a metal toy car
- a child's garden trowel
- a small sieve

- a potato masher
- a metal jug
- a pair of nut crackers
- a small saucepan
- tins with lids

Name: Lovely light and colour
Type of collection: A collection for exploring light and colour
Age group: Three to seven-year-olds

Introduction

As children move on in the Foundation Stage, and then into Key Stage 1, they still need practical activities and real-life objects so they can practise and reinforce their learning. Practice strengthens links between brain cells, making the learning more permanent.

This collection gives children opportunities to explore scientific concepts, in this case, the concepts of light and colour, either separately or together. They are both fascinating concepts for children, and will provide enjoyable, self-initiated tasks, ideal for continuous provision, as well as providing a focus for adult-led sessions, indoors or outside.

Looking through coloured cellophane paper, looking at your own reflection, holding up a glass paperweight, or wearing coloured spectacles all expand children's knowledge and understanding of the world around them. Adding torches, mirrors and kaleidoscopes will extend the fun and the learning, and if you put the basket in a strong light, the children will be able to explore shadows and reflections as well. Hang a light mobile or a prism near the area where the children will be working.

Container

A transparent bucket or a coloured plastic washing-up bowl would be good.

What to collect

Make sure that any glass objects are tough enough to withstand handling.

- a hand mirror
- plastic mirror sheet
- shiny metal bowls
- shiny spoons

- coloured cellophane
- paperweights
- 'snowstorms'
- a telescope

- net or gauze
- cling film
- a kaleidoscope
- bubble wrap

⇨

- small coloured glass jars and bottles
- coloured glass beads
- a piece of curtain net
- clear containers
- small sand timers
- tissue/greaseproof paper
- lametta
- shiny beads
- shiny fabrics
- foil (different colours)

- plastic mirrors
- a jar of bubbles
- plastic bottles filled with coloured liquids
- a torch
- balloons
- shadow puppets
- tinsel
- a tiara
- a crown
- old watches
- shiny buttons

- black paper
- sunglasses
- CD cases
- old glasses frames with cellophane lenses
- a prism
- coloured Perspex
- torches
- strings of lights
- unbreakable Christmas baubles

Useful websites for resources

Spacekraft (www.spacekraft.co.uk) have a wide range of mirrors and light toys. They also sell sensory toys and equipment for children with additional needs. A wide range of materials for exploring light are available from www.tts-group.co.uk.

Using this collection

The collection can be used independently or with adult support.

Taking it further/more ideas

Put the collection on or in front of a mirror to make it even more exciting (www.tts-group.co.uk stock a mirror that fits into a builder's tray).

> **Name**: Put it in
> **Type of collection**: A collection for exploring containers.
> **Age group**: Three to seven-year-olds

Introduction

For younger children, you could start this basket with containers without lids, making for easy access and opening for the younger children. When they have mastered the containers (or for older children) add lids for these containers and some more with hinged lids. You could also offer a range of small bags for the smaller items.

A box enables you to include smaller objects and multiples of things like pasta shapes, beads, coins, stones and shells without losing them.

Some children get very involved in this activity and will spend considerable lengths of time absorbed in it – repeatedly filling and emptying containers. This is a normal stage of development (a schema) – don't stop them!

Container

A large box or basket with a lid. There are lots of wicker, cane and rush storage baskets with lids in home décor shops, and try your local bargain or 'pound shops'.

What to collect

Small items such as:
- small world people
- coins
- beads
- small wooden cars
- large dry pasta shapes
- nuts
- big seeds
- pegs
- metal bottle tops
- keys
- glass 'beads'
- polished stones
- conkers
- acorns
- dried beans
- dried peas
- small brooches and other cheap jewellery

Containers:
- cups
- small plastic bottles
- empty matchboxes
- small tins without lids
- tins with lids
- small bowls
- a small saucepan
- a lid for the saucepan
- boxes (no lids)
- boxes with lids
- purses
- sweet tubes (no top)
- kitchen roll tubes
- a jewellery box
- sorting trays
- bun tins

- paper bun cases
- a spectacle case
- jars with screw tops
- small purses
- a plastic teapot
- small cloth bags
- a watch box
- a ring box
- a pen case
- a wooden box with a hinged lid
- nesting dolls
- an egg box (with wooden eggs)
- small drawstring fabric gift bags
- plastic storage boxes with compartments

Some contents of the box may be specific to one container (such as a ring and a ring box) but don't make it an intelligence test! Let the children choose what goes where.

Useful websites for resources

www.armadillotoys.co.uk sell six wooden eggs in an egg box. www.amazon.co.uk will direct you to lots of different wooden eggs.

Using this collection

This basket rarely needs supervision, as the children get very involved in filling and emptying the containers. However, you could use the resources in an adult-led problem-solving session, or tell stories about the items.

Taking it further/more ideas

Use some of your collection of containers with new objects inside for stimulating discussion in story or language sessions.

Name: Where have we been?
Type of collection: Collections with a focus on the places children have visited
Age group: Three to seven-year-olds

Introduction

This page has suggestions for making baskets to support your work in other areas of learning. You could enhance some of your displays with baskets of objects which are intended to be handled and rearranged!

A sense of place is an important element of Understanding the world, so these baskets give children opportunities to think of real or imagined places. Some could be associated with holidays, others with stories, some with occasions, others with people, and of course many will link with current projects or topics, visits and outings. The secret is to remember that children learn more if they use all their senses, not just sight. Try to include a stimulus for each sense in each collection. Once you start these baskets, the children will suggest more, and you will be able to use your imagination and ingenuity to make a regular feature of such baskets in your setting.

Individual children may like to make baskets to celebrate their holidays or other places they know, and this can be a useful way for them to recall past events in preparation for talking, drawing or writing about what they have done.

Container
Small baskets, or themed containers relevant to the place visited.

Suggestions for what to collect

The hairdresser
- rollers
- hairspray (empty)
- little hotel bottles of shampoo etc
- combs
- brushes
- towels
- hand mirrors
- a book of hairstyles (from magazine photos)
- nail file
- appointment book
- overall

The woods
- leaves, sticks, twigs
- acorns
- conkers
- moss
- stones
- bark
- sawn logs
- small world woodland creatures
- soft toy animals
- books about the woods
- a story about woods – e.g. *The Happy Hedgehog Band* by Martin Waddell and Jill Barton (Walker Books Ltd)

The garden centre (use a garden trug as a container)
- overalls
- gardening gloves
- labels and stickers
- catalogues
- plant pots
- seed catalogues and packets
- small gardening tools
- artificial flowers, leaves
- bulbs
- stones and pebbles
- plant labels
- small world bugs and insects

A useful website for resources
Hopefully you will be able to collect these resources from a visit, but you could also use the internet to find and download lots of pictures for a flipbook of people, animals and objects to add to the basket.

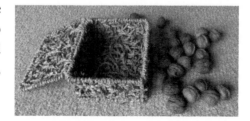

Using this collection
Children can extend their exploration of a recent experience by using the contents of a basket with other 'loose parts' resources, recreating their visit as they do so.

Taking it further/more ideas
Make baskets for the Places of Worship you visit, or for celebrations of all sorts – birthdays, Diwali, Eid, Chinese New Year, weddings and so on.

Name: Our visitor
Type of collection: Collections with a focus on the visitors who have met the children
Age group: Three to seven-year-olds

Introduction

This basket will help children to recall a recent visitor to your setting or school. Handling real objects helps memory, and using all the senses helps too. So include objects with perfumes and textures as well. Younger children will love to use the basket to replay the visit, and older children can use it as a stimulus for talking, drawing and writing.

Container

Small baskets, or themed containers relevant to the visitor.

What to collect

Kay's new baby came

The container could be a baby basket lined with soft fabric, a nappy changing bag or a baby bath.

- a baby doll
- baby clothes
- nappies
- a shawl or baby blanket
- photos of babies
- cards
- baby food jars
- a rattle or baby toys
- a baby bottle
- baby toiletries
- baby equipment catalogues
- a baby feeding bowl and cup
- a baby bath
- baby powder
- bubble bath bottle

Rory the Park Keeper came

The container could be a canvas bag.

- unbreakable thermos
- notebook
- park keeper's cap or hat
- badge
- safety waistcoat
- kid's gardening gloves
- keys for the park gate
- a toy robin
- garden tools
- plant pots
- binoculars
- story of *Percy the Park Keeper* by Nick Butterworth (HarperCollins)
- bird and plant books
- maps and plans of your local park
- photo book
- postcards of parks
- small-world park equipment and people

A useful website for resources

www.hortivation.com sell children's gardening gloves and small gardening tools.

Using these collections

Children love baby play and will be happy to play with the resources independently, but they may be able to recall more in a conversation in a small group supported by an adult.

Rory's bag is best used out of doors to replay his role, adding 'loose parts' and construction materials to recreate the park.

Taking it further/more ideas

When inviting visitors to your setting or school, it can help if you ask them to bring some objects that they use in their lives, and if possible, whether they could leave them for a time for the children to explore.

Name: 'Oh we do like to be beside the seaside!'
Type of collection: A detailed example of a themed collection
Age group: Three to seven-year-olds

Introduction

This is one way that you could expand children's experiences before, during, or after a topic or theme. It isn't possible to include ideas for every topic, just a few examples. This collection would support a topic on Summer, the Seaside or Holidays.

Before starting a new topic, you could offer a collection to get children's ideas going, and remind them of what they already know. During a topic, you could add new items, using the objects as story or discussion starters or provocations to encourage thinking skills. At the end of a topic, the basket should contain reminders of everything you have covered and discussed, and could become a permanent addition to the resources in your room. A photograph of the collection for each topic could be displayed as a reminder of what the children have learned during the year.

Container

A wide container, big enough for several children to explore at the same time.

Alternative containers
A small suitcase, a beach bag, or a backpack.

What to collect

- shells
- stones
- smooth pebbles
- fossils
- real or fake coral
- starfish and other real sea creatures
- small world sea creatures – crabs, fish, starfish etc
- driftwood

- seaweed (real or artificial)
- cork floats
- a book about rock pools
- a bucket
- a swimsuit and towel
- child's mask and flippers
- a beach mat
- sun tan lotion
- sunglasses
- a sunhat

- a fishing net
- some small world people
- small wooden boats
- a camera
- a pirate flag
- a treasure chest and treasure
- a ship in a bottle (or just the bottle)
- binoculars or a telescope

- seaside postcards
- seaside souvenirs such as rock, shell boxes, mugs, 'snowstorms' with scenes inside
- laminated photos of seaside food, treats and souvenirs

Useful websites for resources
www.buythesea-bymail.co.uk; http://marinestore.co.uk for pirate things, treasure chest and flags; www.amazon.co.uk for treasure chests

Using this collection
The resource can be used:

- In a 'thinking session' where adult and children discuss questions such as 'What is this for?' 'What is this made from?' 'How did this get on the beach?'
- As one of the options for continuous provision. Let children feed back their thoughts and stories to the whole group.

Taking it further/more ideas
Introduce some small-world people and a builders' tray of sand for the children to make their own seaside by adding stones, shells, water, boats and so on. Encourage the children to take photos of their creations.

Name: Before me
Type of collection: A collection to encourage exploration of the past
Age group: Three to seven-year-olds

Introduction

This basket helps children to explore the world before they were born, and this does not need to be ancient history! Handling objects that have belonged to family members gives children an early sense of time. These do not need to be museum objects, just things (or even versions of things) that are not in regular use now.

Many can be found in charity shops or jumble sales for a small cost, or you may know of a shop that still sells these things. You could also try asking parents and carers if they or their families have things to donate to your history basket. Schools often have old weights, coins, photos, books and other equipment, and other memorabilia that can add to your collection.

Container

An old basket or bag (try a charity shop). Alternatively use an old fashioned suitcase, a wooden box or a trunk.

What to collect

These are just some suggestions, you and the children will be able to think of more.

Household objects and clothes:

- old cameras
- a lavatory chain and handle
- fabric handkerchiefs
- an apron
- a fountain pen
- old postcards
- a locket
- old photos and pictures
- an old radio
- old crockery, cutlery
- clothes, such as wedding dresses, baby clothes
- braces or a snake belt
- an old blazer

- bicycle clips
- fivestones
- a china teaset
- an old telephone
- knitted baby clothes

Old fashioned toys:
- old board games
- wooden animals
- tin and other metal cars
- an old teddy bear
- an old doll
- clockwork toys
- a slate and chalk

- marbles
- a skipping rope
- a school satchel
- old coins
- baby toys
- rattles
- an old baby doll
- cloth or board books
- a spinning top
- a wooden or rag doll
- old books and annuals
- old toy cars
- TV character dolls

You may also like to add some toys that were around when the children were babies. Looking in your own loft or asking friends and colleagues may be a good source:

- Teletubbies
- Cindy and Barbie
- Cabbage Patch Dolls
- Thunderbirds
- Transformers
- My Little Pony

- Thomas the Tank Engine
- Smurfs
- Sooty
- Bagpuss
- Dangermouse

Resources

Websites are useful for historical objects but the best places are market stalls, junk ships and charity shops, where you should be able to find plenty of things at reasonable prices.

Using this collection

This collection is ideal as a starter to a discussion of what it was like before the children were born. Children love stories and objects from long ago, and this is early history. The collection can also become part of your continuous provision where children can explore the objects alone or with friends.

Name: Light and heavy
Type of collection: A collection to encourage exploration of mass and weight
Age group: Three to seven-year-olds

Introduction

The exploration of weight and mass is an important part of science for young children. This collection should contain:

- objects that are either very light or very heavy

- objects that are big and light, small and heavy
- pairs of objects with different weights
- objects that are very similar in weight.

Physical exploration of the contents of such a basket should come before the abstract concepts of comparison and balance, so don't be tempted to add scales or even balances until the children have mastered the concept of 'heavier and lighter'.

Children of all ages love picking up and handling heavy things and can do this safely if seated on a rug or carpet (or on the grass outside). The lighter things provided can be shaken, waved or tossed in the air. This basket is particularly suited for use out of doors, perhaps on a rug or carpet square, where the light, floaty objects can be watched and enjoyed, and the heavy items will be easier to manage. There is also a place for a variety of gauzy, floaty fabrics, ribbons and streamers, which the children can explore by running, tossing, waving, floating and twirling.

Container
A sturdy container is needed for this collection.

What to collect

- big stones
- a weight from scales
- wood pieces
- a glass paperweight
- tissue paper
- an empty film can
- an empty bean can
- a can of beans
- a paperback and a hardback book
- bubbles
- leaves
- a house brick
- feathers
- paper and china cups
- paper and card
- a plastic bottle
- a glass bottle

- a metal toy car
- a plastic car
- a balloon
- polystyrene
- keys
- polystyrene
- foam
- zip lock bags filled with glass beads, lentils, dried peas, soaked peas, sequins, paper clips, nails, metal washers, dry and wet sand, etc.
- wrap a wooden brick and a plastic brick in paper
- fishermen's weights
- fitness wrist weights
- beanbags

Suitable fabrics
- net
- gauze
- silk
- sari material
- chiffon scarves
- flags and bunting
- crepe paper
- streamers
- bubble wrap
- leather

Using this collection
Exploration needs to come first, then an adult can join the group to extend the discussion of such questions as 'What is light?' 'What is heavy?' 'Why is a bag of dry sand lighter than a bag of wet sand?'

Taking it further/more ideas
This basket could be combined with the 'Will it float?' basket to explore why heavy things sometimes float, and light things can sink.

Name: Will it float?
Type of collection: A collection to encourage exploration of floating and sinking
Age group: Three to seven-year-olds

Introduction
Discuss floating and sinking, waterlogged and flooded with the children and encourage them to use the objects to help with prediction and experimentation. Similar objects (two balls, two cups) one that sinks, one that floats will encourage discrimination and discussion as pairs or groups work independently with this basket. You could also put the basket outside with a bowl of water for experiments.

Of course, you will need to replace those items which disintegrate when immersed!

Container
Try putting a waterproof liner in the basket (or use one designed for plants) in order to reduce the water leakage.

Alternative containers
You could do the experiments in a plastic fish tank or a washing-up bowl.

What to collect

- bubble wrap
- a ping pong ball and a rubber ball
- a metal car and a plastic car
- a plastic cup and an enamel mug
- a plastic Christmas bauble
- conkers, acorns, leaves, walnut
- large and small stones
- feathers

- a pencil
- pieces of different woods – balsa, chipboard, pine etc
- small logs
- cardboard and plastic tubes
- wooden and plastic chopstick
- a sock
- a wooden brick and a plastic brick
- a piece of foam
- polystyrene sheet and 'wiggles'
- coins
- fir cones
- a paper bag
- an apple, an orange and a lemon

- big nails
- buttons
- a golf ball
- a funnel
- china saucer
- paper clips
- elastic bands
- wooden, glass and china beads
- plastic bracelets
- wooden eggs
- corks
- shells
- paper, card and plastic

A useful website for resources

www.underfives.co.uk/float1.html has some good guidance on activities and resources.

Using this collection

Children will enjoy this collection, and if you encourage them, they will find plenty of other things to test! Discussions are important to help children think about why some things float or sink, and what they could do to make a floating thing sink, or vice versa. Making a guess before experimenting (predicting and hypothesising) takes maturity, something that younger children will need help with.

Taking it further/more ideas

Offer two bowls so the children can test, then sort objects into 'things that float' and 'things that sink'.

> **Name**: Sticky magnets!
> **Type of collection**: Another themed collection with a science focus
> **Age group**: Three to seven-year-olds

Introduction

This collection offers free access to scientific exploration. You might want to tie the magnets on to the basket with a long string to make sure they can be easily retrieved.

It would be best not to introduce this activity – just leave the basket for the children to discover, and watch what happens. Some of the objects are small and some are sharp – use your discretion when you assemble the collection, take into account the age and stage of the children and leave out things you are doubtful about. Remember 'when in doubt, leave it out'. You might also like to put this basket on a small table outside.

Container

Plastic container, or basket, a metal bucket might fascinate older children!

What to collect

- a horseshoe magnet
- washers
- tin lids
- paper clips
- small pieces of wood
- a plastic cup
- pencil
- a small plastic bottle
- nails and screws
- nuts and bolts
- drawing pins
- cotton reels
- fir cones
- paper
- wooden shapes
- a stone
- metal badges
- costume jewellery

- a copper bracelet
- a piece of wood
- scissors
- a butter knife
- fridge magnets
- a bicycle bell
- stainless steel spoon or bowl
- coins

Make sure that some of the metal things in the basket cannot be picked up by the magnet! Aluminium items and most coins would be suitable. Some others are:

- a duster
- a nail file
- a shiny plastic bauble
- aluminium objects

Useful websites for resources

www.ascoeducational.co.uk have magnet starter sets with objects and magnets. www.tts-group.co.uk have a wide range of magnets in their science section.

Using this collection

Add this basket to your continuous provision, with or without challenges and provocations. It is suitable for any age from three to seven, but will need more challenges to keep older children engaged.

Taking it further/more ideas

Add some different sorts of magnets, barrel magnets, bar magnets, magnetic strip, magnet games, even floating magnets and magnetic beads. Or add a baking tray and some magnetic letters.

Name: Sort the sound
Type of collection: Phonic treasure baskets
Age group: Three to seven-year-olds

Introduction

The 'loose parts' approach is particularly suited to introducing phonic collections – using single sounds at first. Encourage the children to contribute to the phonic baskets and give a clue by hanging a clear, unambiguous picture label on the edge of the basket. A snake is unambiguous – a sweet could be confusing for some children!

Use your discretion and knowledge of the children in your group to decide whether you could use two baskets at once or several over a week – double baskets may not be appropriate before the Reception year and may be very stressful for children who are learning English as an additional language.

Container

Small baskets are best, so you can have more than one on the go at once. After use you might want to keep the collections in plastic bags for future use.

What to collect
Here are two examples:

An 's' basket might contain:	A 'b' basket might contain:
• a sandal	• a badge
• a can of soup	• a ball
• a snake	• some buttons
• a saucepan	• a bowl
• a snail shell	• a toy bike
• a stamp	• binoculars
• a skittle	• a brick
• scissors	• a box
• a slipper	• a belt
• a seed	• a baby's bib
• a strawberry	• a bandage
• a stone	• a bucket
• a spoon	• a string of beads
• a spider	• a fabric or metal butterfly
• a brooch & bracelet	• a biscuit
• sequins	• a plastic bauble
• a sweet	• a little basket

The Little Book of Phonics by Sally Featherstone (Bloomsbury/Featherstone) has suggestions for baskets for every initial sound and some digraphs.

Using this collection
Start with single sounds and then use more than one basket during a week, letting the children explore the contents after a group session with an adult. Let the children help to collect the contents for the basket – this can be a useful start to finding out how their phonological awareness is developing.

You could combine the contents of two baskets for a phonic sorting activity, offering the children two smaller baskets to sort the things into as they name them. Children with English as an additional language may find the baskets of objects very helpful in naming and in developing listening skills.

Taking it further/more ideas
Make an alphabet basket, with objects for each letter sound, and use it with an alphabet mat, indoors or outside.

Name: What's the difference?
Type of collection: Baskets to support thinking and creativity
Age group: Three to seven-year-olds

Introduction

This type of basket gives children opportunities to compare and sort, discussing as they do so. These baskets can either contain one type of object (for instance a collection of watches, or things with holes), or a mixture of objects. It's useful to restrict the range

of objects offered, so the basket does not become just a random collection, which can be confusing for children when they are comparing and contrasting objects.

Children will enjoy contributing to the collection by bringing objects from home or from around the room and in the garden.

When you introduce a new basket or contents, be careful that you don't imply that there is only one 'right' way to use it. Keep your introduction brief, saying you have put some new things in the basket, and show them where it will be if they want to use it. Let them explore and discover.

Container

The same basket can be used over and over again for different collections. If you do this, the children will get used to the idea of a 'thinking basket'. One with a lid will add to the thinking.

What to collect

Collections to sort	Big and small	Things with holes	Squares, rectangles and cubes
watches	gloves, socks,	beads	bricks
keyrings	t-shirts, shoes	CDs	boxes
necklaces and bracelets	toy cars	washers	stock cubes
big beads	keys	rings	dice
large seeds and nuts	teddies	pasta	envelopes
cutlery (not knives)	lids	buttons	CD cases
coins	plastic bottles	washers	matchboxes
shells	keys	beads	little gift boxes
stones and pebbles	nails and screws	sequin waste	

⇨

glass beads	boxes	cotton reels	cylinders
clothing	tins	nuts and bolts	straws
	washers		tubes
	balls		tubing
	marbles		corks
	saucers		empty cans
	buttons		big candles
	stones and shells		empty tablet tubs
	boxes		tops from aerosols
			hair rollers
			snack tubes

A useful website for resources

The best place to find these things is a charity shop or car boot sale!

Using this collection

Let the children explore the objects freely, either alone or with an adult. Try not to impose your ideas about sorting or arranging the objects, let them come up with their own ideas.

Taking it further/more ideas

Use the same box or basket with just one item – an unfamiliar fruit, a natural object such as a big shell, an item of clothing, a tiny cup or spoon, an ornament, a bag of coins. Let the children explore and talk about the objects and then decide what it might be, who it belongs to and where it was found.

Name: Shapes without names
Type of collection: Another example of a basket to support thinking and creativity
Age group: Three to seven-year-olds (matched to the age and experience of the children).

Introduction
This is a true heuristic basket. It contains objects that have no clear purpose or even names. In this basket you can put all sorts of objects that children can explore and use freely, with no expected outcome. Of course the contents need to match the stage of development of the children.

Container
Try to find an unusual container, such as a special wooden box, a picnic basket with a lid, a velvet bag. Use this container each time you present the children with a new collection to explore.

Some things to collect
As with a treasure basket, a mixed bag is often more successful than a collection of one thing.

- pieces of wood (driftwood has a lovely texture and many different shapes)
- smooth irregular offcuts of softwood
- unusual stones and pebbles
- bark pieces
- pieces of broken pottery
- foam or polystyrene shapes
- unusual fruit and vegetables
- packaging shapes
- natural sponges and corks
- metal bits and pieces
- sea glass, smoothed by the sea
- plastic 'jewels' of all sizes and shapes
- unusual shaped pieces of plastic
- bottles and jars
- little abstract carvings

A useful website for resources
You will find these collections more difficult to purchase in shops, and may have to collect the objects over time, adding them as you find them. You could try www.ebay.co.uk for driftwood pieces, and charity shops for some other objects.

Using this collection
Let the children explore the objects or choose one each to talk about in a small group. Let the conversation flow freely, only asking questions if the discussion flags.

You could talk about what the objects remind you of, who they belong to, what they are called.

Taking it further/more ideas

Encourage the children to add objects as they find them – on walks, at home, or when out with their family. Foreign holidays are a good source of unfamiliar objects.

Add some objects that the children might not recognise, such as a wooden lemon squeezer, a honey dipper, unusual spoons, pieces of unusual jewellery and so on.

Maintenance and Storage

6

Looking carefully at the objects you choose

When collecting or buying objects for treasure baskets or heuristic play, look at them carefully before deciding whether or not to include them. Carry out regular risk assessments of objects, particularly those used by babies, who will mouth everything. Carrying out a risk assessment does not, however, mean restricting children's access to a wide range of everyday materials and objects to explore. We must be vigilant (that is why adults must be on hand, particularly when young babies are using treasure baskets), but not so cautious that we remove all interest, texture and colour.

Reasonable risks

There are reasonable risks for all babies and children, and your managers will be able to advise you on the policy for your setting or school. However, we must allow babies and children to have access to natural materials and later to 'loose parts'. A life led in a totally risk-free, man-made environment may

well end up in children taking unacceptable risks later in life, because they have not been trained to handle objects sensibly and safely. Older children should be introduced to new materials in a group situation where risks can be explained.

Regular maintenance

As with any resource, you must make sure that regular cleaning and maintenance takes place. It isn't good enough to just assume that 'someone will do it'. There must be a clear responsibility, either assigned to one of the staff, or listed with the programme of regular cleaning. This may be easier to arrange in a nursery, where practitioners are trained in safe practice of play materials, but adults working with older children should still be conscious of potential risks.

Some frequently asked questions

1 **I'm worried about the babies swallowing things.** If you are worried about any of the things you choose to include in a basket, put the object in your own mouth. If you can't swallow it, then neither can the baby. Buying a choke tester is a sensible precaution (see page 28 and Chapter 7, page 113 for suppliers). 'If in doubt, leave it out' is a good motto – there are plenty of other objects to choose from.

2 **What about the long handles?** Small babies are very careful with the objects they handle. The risk increases as they get a bit older and start to test things by banging, scraping and poking with them. Watch the children, and if you become concerned, remove long-handled objects or cut the handles down.

3 **And fruit?** Items such as fruit (and paper items) need to be replaced as soon as they look worn – otherwise a treasure basket will soon lose its appeal.

4 **Why do you suggest using tin cans that might have sharp edges?** These are a free resource and children love using them! They make a good sound when rolled or when you drop things in them. When collecting these, make sure that you check them, and all other metal items, for sharp edges, pressing these down with the handle of a serving spoon, and covering the edges with duct tape. Then check tins regularly for sharp edges and corners, and feel wooden objects for splinters and other wear and tear. Treasure baskets need this regular check as well, and any items that cause concern should be discarded.

5 **'Loose parts' resources are just junk – isn't this dangerous for children?** 'Loose parts' are by nature very varied, and 'real-life objects' are not as 'safe' as those manufactured, tested and sold specifically for children's use. However,

these materials offer so many opportunities for learning that it would be very unfortunate if practitioners and teachers felt uneasy about their use.

6 **What about the germs?** Anything that can be washed, should be washed regularly, preferably in a dishwasher. Items that cannot be immersed in water need wiping with a damp cloth and disinfectant. Some objects (but not metal ones) can be sterilised by putting them in a microwave.

A note on storage

If you collect objects over time, you can have one or more treasure baskets in use at any time, you can combine collections and make up new ones. When not in use, the objects can be stored in the baskets, but this can cause problems if they don't stack securely, and of course, the baskets themselves can be an expense.

Practitioners in settings where treasure baskets are regularly in use find it more convenient to store items not currently being used in one of the following ways:

- labelled boxes with lids, one for each collection
- drawstring fabric bags which can be hung on the back of a door or in a cupboard
- plastic stacking crates or boxes (a cheaper option, but more likely to attract dust!)
- plastic transparent 'book bags' (the advantage being that you can see the contents).

Heuristic play resources are already stored in their own bags, and these can be hung neatly out of the way in a cupboard or even on the wall of your room.

'Loose parts' materials sometimes present a more complex storage task. There are some suggestions in Chapter 5, see page 64, and in the resources chapter at the end of the book. Trolleys, sets of drawers, and other simple, accessible storage are a must for these resources, so the children can see and select what they need for their play without asking an adult.

Costs

Heuristic play collections can be very cost-effective resources, particularly if you collect them over time. The majority of the contents in the treasure baskets and heuristic play collections in this book will cost you only small amounts to buy, and many are free. If you have limited funds, concentrate on one or two well-stocked baskets, a smaller number of play bags, or smaller items from the list of 'loose parts'. Your children will have just as much fun with these. Remember:

- Some objects are free – collected on walks and excursions, recycled from 'junk', or donated by parents, staff and friends.
- Some are cheap, acquired from charity shops or in sales.
- Some are pieces of household equipment made to last.
- Some can be sourced via the internet, where bargains can be found in return for a bit of searching.
- Some (relatively few) will need to be bought specially, or regularly replaced. However, there are now far more suppliers of heuristic play materials and we have included some of these in Chapter 7 in Resources and Suppliers, see page 109.

Early years practitioners are inventive and always on the lookout for a bargain or free objects, a substitute or an alternative. Just hold on to the principles of this type of play. The objects should be:

- everyday, easily-found objects
- natural
- clean and safe in use
- checked and replaced regularly.

And always remember that heuristic play of all sorts should encourage children to use of all their senses, introduce them to a wide range of natural materials, providing the subtle colours, textures and shapes of natural objects to balance the current use of bright colours and man-made materials. The activities should stimulate free-choice play and provide opportunities for them to make choices and develop preferences from a very young age, in the company of supportive, caring adults.

Above all, heuristic play should be enjoyable, engaging fun for children and adults!

7 Books and Resources

Books

Caring Spaces, Learning Places: children's environments that work Jim Greenman (Exchange Press, 1998)

Developing Play for the Under 3s: the treasure basket and heuristic play Anita M. Hughes (Routledge, 2010)

Heuristic Play: Play in the EYFS Sheila Riddall-Leech (Practical Pre-school, 2009)

Outdoor Play: Play in the EYFS Sue Durrant (Practical Pre-school, 2009)

People Under Three Elinor Goldschmeid and Sonia Jackson (Routledge 2003)

Sensory World: progression in play for babies and children Sally Featherstone, Liz Williams (A&C Black/Featherstone, 2006)

Sensory Play: Play in the EYFS Sue Gascoyne (Practical Pre-school, 2011)

The Little Book of Treasure Baskets Sally Featherstone, Ann Roberts (A&C Black/Featherstone, 2002)

Setting the Scene: creating successful environments for babies and young children Sally Featherstone (A&C Black/Featherstone, 2011)

The Natural World: progression in play for babies and children Sally Featherstone (A & C Black/Featherstone, 2006)

Understanding Child Development Jennie Lindon (Hodder, 2010)

Video/DVD

Exploratory Play Siren Films http://www.sirenfilms.co.uk

Heuristic Play with Objects: children of 12–20 months exploring everyday objects. DVD; Elinor Goldschmied and Anita Hughes http://resources.ncb.org.uk (1992)

Infants at Work: babies of 6–9 months exploring everyday objects. Elinor Goldschmied http://resources.ncb.org.uk (1992)

Other references

Forest Schools www.forestschools.com

Scrapstores www.scrapstoresuk.org

The Secret Garden Nursery www.secretgardenoutdoor-nursery.co.uk/

Suppliers and sources for equipment and storage

Baskets

Circular storage basket	www.englishwillowbaskets.co.uk	Basket only	
Treasure basket	www.designsforeducation.co.uk	Basket and storage bag	
Treasure basket	www.thetreasurebasket.co.uk	Basket only	
Treasure basket	www.designsforeducation.co.uk	Basket only	

Filled baskets

	www.heritagetreasurebaskets.co.uk	Four different collections	36 objects
	www.playtoz.co.uk	For baskets, collections, training and other resources.	
	www.ascoeducational.co.uk		50 objects
	www.theconsortium.co.uk	With cards	25 objects
	www.earlyexcellence.com		

Collections for your own basket

A range of collections.	www.earlyexcellence.com	
A range of different baskets eg natural, rhythm, shiny etc.	www.finesolutions.co.uk	Enough objects for one baby
	www.finesolutions.co.uk	Group set

Objects suitable for heuristic play (treasure baskets and bags)

Starter set	www.costcuttersuk.com	70 pieces
Starter set	www.millwoodeducation.co.uk	70 plus objects
Starter set	www.earlyyearsathome.co.uk	63 objects
Starter set	www.consortiumcare.co.uk	63 plus items
Starter set	www.thewholekaboodle.com	78 pieces

⇨

Curtain rings, bowls, balls, beads and other shapes.	www.earlyexcellence.com	Sets of 12
Split dried oranges.	www.earlyyearsathome.co.uk	Bag of six
Wooden ring stand.	www.earlyyearsathome.co.uk	
Pack of corks.	www.thewholekaboodle.com	
Small wooden bowls.	www.superstickers.com	Bag of four

Useful websites for objects

Scrapstores are located all over the country, look up your area on the website. They have a range of objects that are waste, but safe to use. You may have to pay an annual fee, but after that the resources are free.	www.scrapstoresuk.org
Large bags of natural objects (cones, seed heads, cane balls, dried oranges).	www.galt-educational.co.uk
Laces, ribbon lengths, wooden spools, feathers, dolly pegs, craft sticks, buckets of shells, buttons.	www.thewholekaboodle.com
13 piece stainless steel, child-sized, kitchen set.	www.kidscopeeducation.co.uk
The Wool Company sell baby blankets and baby sheepskins.	http://www.thewoolcompany.co.uk
Wooden rings, egg cups, balls.	www.superstickers.com
Stainless steel balti dishes, wooden doorknobs, big beads, pet bowls.	www.ebay.co.uk
Stainless steel cat dishes.	www.petplanet.co.uk
Rubber doorstops.	www.handles4doors.co.uk
Window wedge, pack of three. Doorwedge, rubber. Doorstops, pack of two.	www.toolsandhardwaredirect.co.uk
Plain charity wristbands.	www.britanniapromotionuk.co.uk
Plain wristbands.	www.charitypromotionuk.com
Wooden doorknobs.	www.poshknob.co.uk

Wooden curtain rings.	www.diy.com (B&Q)
Cabinet doorknobs.	www.ironmongerydirect.co.uk
Woolen pompoms. also soft string, big buttons, cotton thread.	www.bloomingfelt.co.uk
Cane bag handles for treasure baskets.	www.texere-yarns.co.uk
Strong card hosiery yarn cones. Variety yarn packs. Also a huge variety of yarns of different types.	www.texere-yarns.co.uk
Nesting sets of boxes.	www.ikea.com
Empty wooden spools. Also bags of natural and mixed coloured feathers, lolly sticks, dolly pegs, artificial leaves, pipe cleaners.	www.curtisward.com
Shells – 60 moon or 50 cockle shells plus a wide selection of unusual shells, single and in bags.	www.buythesea-bymail.co.uk
More shells and seaside objects.	www.onlineshells.co.uk/
All sorts of corks. Also cork balls, place mats and coasters. Look for the clearance bit where they have odd sizes and shapes.	www.just-cork.co.uk
Plastic topped corks (packs of 100). Crown caps (packs of 100). Straight corks (packs of 30). Plastic wine corks (packs of 25). Plus other stoppers and caps.	www.brewsmarter.co.uk
Cheap small baskets, some lined with plastic; artificial flowers and leaves; glass beads.	www.thebaggery.co.uk or other floristry suppliers
Little coloured metal buckets.	www.countrybaskets.co.uk
Very large vintage beads, worth considering buying a few!	www.jewelsandfinerycraft.co.uk
Individual large wooden beads.	www.regalcrafts.com
Natural wooden tree blocks (packs of 35). Coloured beads in bags (packs of 30).	www.myriadonline.co.uk

⇨

Plain wooden eggs (packs of 15).
Compressed cotton eggs (packs of 200).
Dolly pegs (packs of 30).
Mini tin pails in sets (packs of 12).
Jingle bells (packs of 50).
Sequin waste; raffia; packs of keyrings;
sorting pots and trays; craft sticks and other
wooden craft supplies.

www.littlecraftybugs.co.uk

Small wooden figures (packs of six).

www.communityplaythings.co.uk

Mirrors and light toys, sensory toys and
equipment for children with additional
needs.

http://www.spacekraft.co.uk

This supplier stocks a fantastic range of
sensory and tactile fabrics, plus bags, and
baskets with two handles, suitable for
outdoor collections.

www.dickorydockdesigns.co.uk

Kaleidoscopes for children.

www.aspace.co.uk

Fabric bags, mirrors, light toys, collections
of natural materials, pebbles, feathers,
shells, sponges, moss, translucent slices of
rock, and much more.

www.tts-group.co.uk/

Musical instruments, cookery equipment,
wooden toys.

www.spottygreenfrog.co.uk

Baskets and objects for older children

PSED baskets.

www.earlyexcellence.com

Story baskets (filled).

www.earlyexcellence.com

Storage

The website of a nursery nurse who makes
strong, high quality drawstring bags as a
hobby.

www.sacks-n-stories.co.uk

Drawstring bags

There are hundreds of promotional gift sites on
the internet. Try some to see if they will provide
bags without logos!

Cheap hessian sacks

http://www.potloads.com

Hessian and cotton drawstring bags.

http://thecleverbaggers.co.uk

Zip up bags – one side clear one side coloured (packs of six).	www.designsforeducation.co.uk
Sorting trays, various sizes.	www.tts-group.co.uk
Hundreds of different storage boxes and towers.	www.reallyusefulproducts.co.uk
Laundry bags in a range of colours.	www.washingnet.org.uk
Supermarket shopping baskets. Wheeled shopping baskets suitable for outdoor use.	www.storagesystemsdirect.co.uk

Miscellaneous

Safety 1st small object Choking Tests.	www.amazon.co.uk
Babydan choke tester.	www.safetots.co.uk
Choke Tube Tester.	www.onestepahead.com